POP AS ART

POP as ART

A Survey of the New Super Realism

by Mario Amaya

STUDIO VISTA, LONDON

to C.F.J. with gratitude

© 1965 Mario Amaya

Published in London by Studio Vista Limited,
Blue Star House, Highgate Hill, N 19
Reprinted in 1966
Set in 12 pt D Garamond 1 pt leaded

Made and printed in the Netherlands by Koch en Knuttel, Gouda

CONTENTS

To write a study of an art movement while it is still in the throes of its development may seem presumptuous, if not foolhardy. But so-called 'Pop Art' or the New Super Realism has created such widespread confusion, dissension, admiration, and popular attention in so short a life-span that such a book might be helpful in describing the atmosphere in which it has developed, and in reflecting some of the ideas currently expounded about it at the time of its inception.

The new art has had instant fame and an instant success, unlike any other movement in modern art. It is self-confessed to being an instant art form, for an instant society, and as such lends itself to instant art history. No other contemporary movement has had so much written about it so soon, or has lent itself so readily to the quick-fix documentary approach.

Among the many articles attempting to detail a movement as diverse and full of changes as Pop Art, perhaps the most successful have been those in which interviews with the artists gauged direct, personal reactions to their work as it was being created. G. R. Swenson's series for *Art News* are the most often quoted and were an invaluable help in writing this book. Catalogues and articles by Alan R. Solomon of the Jewish Museum, Lawrence Alloway of the Guggenheim, and Henry Geldzahler of the Metropolitan Museum, all in New York, were equally stimulating and provided many points of discussion, as well as departure. Jasia Reichardt's historical survey of British Pop Art in *Art International* was an essential source, as were Richard Smith's articles in *Ark*, Richard Hamilton's writings, John Cage's book *Silence* as well as his many catalogue notes, pieces by Barbara Rose, Robert Rosenblum, Max Kozloff, David Sylvester, D. G. Seckler, Ellen H. Johnson, Donald Judd, Ivan Karp, and John Ashbery. And Leo Steinberg's idiosyncratic monograph on Jasper Johns prompted much thought.

The publishers and myself are most grateful to the Walker Art Center, Minneapolis for the loan of certain colour blocks for this book. Other acknowledgements are made beneath the pictures.

It is almost impossible to define Pop Art in any strict sense, the way one can define, say, Cubism or Surrealism. Therefore, the selection of artists included in this book is bound to be somewhat arbitrary and disputable. However, I have concentrated on those artists mostly in America and Great Britain who either use the techniques and processes of commercial art for aesthetic purposes, or through a painterly approach reflect commercially inspired ad-mass references.

Thus, not only the means but the aims and ends have been taken into consideration in the selection made, with the full knowledge that most of the artists strongly deny they are 'Pop', seldom admit that they have anything at all in common, and resist being grouped into any sort of a style or even a movement.

NEW YORK, 1965   *Mario Amaya*

Forms ought to have the emotion of a concrete experience. For instance, I am very happy to see that grass is green. At one time, it was very daring to make a figure red or blue - I think now that it is just as daring to make it flesh-coloured.

Willem de Kooning

I   The Ad-Mass Scene

Never before has the human eye been so assaulted by images printed, painted, photographed, stencilled, and otherwise copied, both moving and still. Because of the immense power and spread of advertising and mass-media communications through publications and television since the Second World War, we have taken for granted a whole new set of signs, symbols, emblems and imagery, which has settled into our subconscious as a commonly shared visual experience. Such immediately recognizable objects and images, mass–produced to a numbing degree, have become part of a mid-twentieth-century urban 'folk' art, made not by the many but by the anonymous few; not by the naive and untrained but by the suprasophisticated; not for enlightenment and pleasure but for materialistic and commercial ends. As hideous, vulgar, repulsive, and cheap as some of them may appear, these commercial artifacts constitute a new potent means of visual communication and the Pop artist is concerned with scrutinising this strange new language. It is not surprising that young artists who have grown up in such surroundings, and who in fact know no others, should be interested in exploiting the psychological, sociological, mythological (as well as purely visual) elements in such images, taking them out of context, transforming them and elevating them to the level of 'fine art'.

Whereas the Abstract Expressionist of a previous generation relied on his subconscious and his alienation from a hostile society to demonstrate a personal gesture on the canvas-arena, the new art relies for visual and emotional impact on widely accepted trivia of the commonplace world, as seen and understood through movies, television, comic strips, newspapers, girlie magazines, 'glossies', high fashion, car styling, billboards and other forms of advertising. Rather than value art exclusively as something separate and distinct from life, these young artists have begun to see it as something inspired by the ready-made, fresh from the assembly line, as it enters everyday reality. Direct experience and primary emotion are eschewed for the manufactured, gift-wrapped feeling, shiny and new and guaranteed not to tarnish. These artists are not painting about 'life' itself so much as about an ad-mass attitude to a way of living, as experienced through certain commercial idioms.

Such art, by its very nature, is transitory. Its freshness, its excitement, its uniqueness depend on quick change, newness for its own sake, the expendable, the gimmicky, the cheap, the mass-produced, the deliberately offensive or ugly: in fact all the things which we have been taught to abhor in a work of art.

The new art is not a style so much as a shared point of view about the modern environment, sexy, sensational and saleable, which has sprung up during the last twenty-five years in Europe and particularly in America. Its artists, many of whom never knew of each other's existence until they had been lumped together as a movement, emerged from all parts of the United States and Great Britain, and a few from the Continent; but all of them were drawn to the great focal point of contemporary civilisation – the giant megalopolis.

This is an urban art. It is for the city and about the city and it seems significant that it has developed most completely in the Western World's two biggest, most commercial, extravagant and busy capitals: London and New York. In such cities, where millions must serve and be served by the industrial machine on an equal basis daily, such art seems to direct attention towards the strange, inhuman, synthetic elements that man has produced, not for basic existence, but as a by-product of it. The pre-fabricated, plastic reality of a package existence, as it arrives after endless processing through Madison Avenue, the glossy magazines, and multiple stores, has more meaning than the product it contains. In fact, the entire image of the commodity has been commercially transformed before it gets to us: bread becomes Wonderloaf, cereal becomes Snap, Crackle and Pop. This has further overtones when the same brand packages offer coupons that urge us to procure additional, un-necessary ephemera such as celluloid 'lace' table-mats and plastic roses. Every-thing comes in a box: our job, our pleasures, our dreams, our love life.

Visual enjoyment is equally indirect: movies are appreciated more than live theatre, and television more than movies; the first distils the second and has its final popular success on the third. Works of art become colour reproductions, and many cannot see the difference between the two. Newspapers give us our literature through the photograph which describes sex, slander and horror in the same even tone; by overstressing morality while defying it, the press has reduced the 'immoral' to a meaningless commodity – something to be sold like Wonderloaf. Sex itself is over-blown and exaggerated beyond the limits of belief, until the visual symbols them-selves of a Diana Dors or a Steve Reeves turn into figures of fantasy.

PETER PHILLIPS: CUSTOM PAINTING, 1962. *Oil on canvas, background silver. Courtesy of the artist, New York.*

ANTHONY DONALDSON: IT WON'T BE LONG NOW, 1964.
Oil on canvas, 66" × 66". Courtesy Rowan Gallery, London.

It is a peculiar, twisted world that the artist sees today if he bothers to look. John Gunther has written: 'There have been more changes in the past sixty-five years than in all other centuries put together. No longer do most people believe in the orderly progression of cause and effect; no longer do they believe in the natural goodness of man and the inevitability of progress. Stability has gone. This is an era of quibble, doubt and qualm. Science, technology, art, architecture, music, literature have all acquired new values and revolutionary conflicts rage.'

In contrast to the world's increasing confusion and change, both in values and in society, the artist at the same time witnesses a suffocating standardisation and specialisation; life is no longer accepted as a whole *in continuo*, but fragmented into a thousand divided occupations, in which human beings become so many cogs in bureaucracy's churning wheel, and where everything is governed not by the mind but by the machine. Life itself is threatened less by the almost mythical Bomb, than by the terrifying spread of urbanisation. It is under all these conditions that the artist realises the fact that our five senses today receive feeling, opinion and fact in a totally different way than ever before. And it is by grasping some elements in all these changes, that he himself desires to change – that is, if his work is to remain viable and meaningful, and is to justify its own existence.

The increase of what has become known as 'popular culture' over the last quarter of a century has been phenomenal. The paperback boom alone would be enough to cite a remarkable revolution, but there are also television, picture magazines and movies. The less sophisticated or refined 'popular arts', with a whole new breed of mass-culture editors, writers and commercial artists, become more demanding and oppressive in their levelling down of thought, genius and individuality.

Some believe, because of this, that the so-called 'fine arts' are made redundant and unnecessary in the twentieth century by technological progress, but while 'popular arts' prevail in gigantic quantities, there is also a demand for the 'fine art' product as a desirable ideal more than as a need. In fact, never before has a demand for Art with a capital A been so large, and yet never before have so few people known what to expect from a work of art, or indeed, had less idea as to what it should be. Art washes over them like a giant beach-wave: they learn of it through the millions of magazines, through the hypnotic dazzle of a jumping television screen, through badly-coloured reproductions of 'modern masters'. They move like stunned sheep through galleries trying to see not what they think they should see but what others tell them to see: they rarely look at the works, but enjoy looking at themselves looking at the works. Art has become separated, divorced from life, something special for the walls of an institution and only to be visited on rare occasions. It is not for the home but for the public place; not for a personal experience, but for a group event. The constant flow of changing exhibitions, the quick glimpse of illustrations, the continuous novelty presented as the latest thing, all create an impression that art must of necessity be different, new, impermanent and inexplicable. All this might have little to do with the true artist, or his desire to search out new styles or anti-styles which express more strongly his feelings about his civilisation. It is only when a group of artists actually *use* the popular culture itself as straight source material, and thus directly accept its visual existence, that the old division between 'popular' and 'fine' art must be questioned. By accepted definition today, anything is a fit subject for art, but if one takes the corollary to mean one can make art out of what has always been considered the direct antithesis of art, and consequently produce a work which looks to an untrained eye like something you see every day in the supermarket, a very curious situation arises. One is forced to rethink the entire concept of what art is, and what it can be; and one must reconsider how much of a role the artist has to play in the transformation or quotation before it becomes accepted as a 'work of art'. Moreover, if popular art is to be seen as fine art through the medium of the artist, does its acceptance ultimately depend on the decision of the prestige commercial gallery, or the vagaries of a modern museum official? Or can we decide for ourselves, without agreed values or standards, at what point the artist has entered the inner sanctum of fine art or whether he is still in the open fields of commercial art? With artists themselves using every known commercial process to 'make' their work more and more like a manufactured commodity, the problems become manifold.

As far as the artist is concerned, much of this undoubtedly has to do with his own feelings about his new role in a society where art has become smart. Traditionally the artist has been the ignored producer, appreciated when it was too late, misunderstood, isolated from his culture. Today's artist is 'with it' not only in terms of his 'popular' subject matter but by his new status in society as a celebrity figure, sought after, lionised, interviewed, photographed. His success is not so different from that of the movie star: he may be taken up or dropped at a moment's notice, he is subject to changing fashion, he must constantly be in the foreground and ahead of the game. This leads to a sort of performance-artist, who works in almost direct relationship to the commercial art world, who produces for exhibitions rather than for himself, who tries to anticipate the expectations of powerful critics and dealers, and who must create attention at all costs or perish in a sea of thousands of other artists, all fighting to reach the raft of success.

If the so-called Pop artists have responded to this reality without cover-up, by using all the tricks of commercial sales technique, advertising art and press-agentry to make their impact, they are not only making use openly of what others practise secretly, but are also making an implicit comment on what art today is about. In addition, by using mechanical processes which themselves might spell the death of fine art forever, and by using materials which are self-destructive through their own perishability, are they not consciously defying the gallery system that is based on the unique item and the durability of the sales product?

An obsession with everything that fine art is supposed not to be directs them; yet, this is not a statement against art as such. Nor is it a declaration for anything else, beyond the right to refuse any pre-conceived limitations in art. Such artists accept the despicable, with a terrible *sang froid*, and in a way that declares they are neither hating nor loving, but just having. Instead of taking up the fight against mass-think, they have repeated it, parrot-like, in their own works, over and over again until it sinks into the spectator's sensibilities as a thing with which he must come to terms as best he can. They do not romanticise, or beautify, and seldom indulge in sentimental nostalgia, but work in a no-man's-land they call the 'gap' between life and art, where feelings and handiwork are restricted to what has been done or felt by others. They want nothing to do with the past, as they attempt to grasp some understanding of the present, and in the commonplace of everyday existence their own *raison d'être* is that they hope to make ordinary banalities take on a new, mysterious, totemic meaning.

This type of aesthetic accepts things exactly as they are: ordinary surroundings are looked at from an outward, objective viewpoint and without embarrassment – often with a sense of wonder, curiosity and pleasure, sometimes with irony and fun. Thus, in examining a tube of toothpaste, a soup tin, the piled up accumulation of a supermarket or an Automat, the myth of a Marilyn or that of a Liz, a plastic display hamburger or a matchbook cover, these artists can often project a new sense of the visual jetsam that daily assaults our eyes and minds. Moreover, they indirectly bring into focus the kind of society we all accept without too much complaint.

But, whatever might be implied by the subject matter, such artists are not offering explicit social comment or political protest. The subject matter is there because that is how they found it. They are cool, detached and passive in their acceptance of these visual facts, as cool and detached as a brave new world that accepts an H-bomb as a means of peace. This is their age, an age of contradiction, compromise and ambiguity in which they paranoiacally search for security, sated with overproduction, leisure and waste; an age when to be amoral is often the ultimate in morality, where a truer sense of beauty can often be found only in the ugly, where the mass-produced is more telling than the unique, and where ironies are more meaningful than tragedies. All this is expressed in their work. And here, even the creative act, the last vestige of individuality and non-conformism in an increasingly mechanised culture, is itself proclaimed as dehydrated, as mechanical and as processed as a pre-cooked TV Dinner, yet important as such.

So careful an examination of the commonplace reminds one of the child who is constantly puzzled by things but never doubts their existence or refuses to accept them as interesting. It is like an infant who, discovering some object, perhaps a cup or a saucepan or an ashtray, will pick it up, study it for a long time and then exclaim triumphantly, 'Look!' It is the 'simple game of naming things – one at a time', as Dore Ashton describes it; an act much denigrated in our time and one that has been heavily criticised as pointless and unrewarding. But if looking at reality has become so automatic, perfunctory and redundant, perhaps this is just the moment to begin once more – particularly when those things around us can provide a new visual stimulus which communicates in a variety of ways a whole set of new customs and realities of the visible world.

Because of the cross-reference between the new art's subjects and objects, taken from 'popular culture', it has been called Pop Art, but no term could be more misleading or create more misunderstanding. One of the few things, however, that justifies the title is that, ironically, it has actually become popular since 1962. Although it began as a highly sophisticated art comment on some visual facts in the world of mass-media, it was never intended for the masses themselves or made specifically to be understood by the many rather than the few.

But because of the power and immediacy of its imagery, borrowed from an over-developed system of commercial art, it has reached the public at large through an endless number of articles, television discussions, and reproductions in both the popular press and the glossies and by Madison Avenue itself, which has cleverly absorbed for its own ends what it initially inspired.

Therefore it has strangely been confused with the reference to 'popular culture' that prompted Lawrence Alloway to invent the term 'Pop Art' in London in 1954. The confusion was compounded when Mr. Alloway himself extended his label in 1962 to include artists who dealt with the popular image in a fine art context.

Moulded into a movement by its detractors and its admirers, the new painting and object-making has been given a variety of other names, none of them accurate, few of them in any way suitable: New Realism, Neo-Dada, *Le Nouveau Réalisme*, Sign Painting, New Vulgarianism, and Commonism. Pop Art, its most catchy description, seems to have stuck.

A better name suggested might be the New Super Realism. This alludes not only to a new type of realism which has nothing to do with that of the past, but to the super elements in our culture: the supermarket, supermen idols, the supersales directive, the super-sophistication of a super-saturated society that values the new for its own sake. It also employs the two most overworked adjectives in advertising. Moreover, it indicates the large scale these artists employ within a forced size, which goes beyond mere reality and at the same time is rooted in it, as well as the continual search for the ephemeral, the changing, the sensational. Superrealism, a term used by Sir Herbert Read to describe what later became known as Surrealism, is also to some degree a source, but there is no direct connection between them.

The New Super Realism is one of the few contemporary art phenomena – if not the only one – that has filtered down to the 'plebs' almost immediately. Not since the time of the *Salon* artists and Academicians of the nineteenth century, has an art been as widely embraced by a majority of people. In an era when dozens of new styles and fads compete for attention, this has particular significance. The New Super Realism curiously seems to have provided some common meeting ground on which the issues of today's art can be brought home with greater vigour and point. This does not necessarily speak for its value or quality, or even for its lasting interest and importance. It merely supports the fact that if it can capture the imagination of the specialist, dilettante and man in the street, then it is of importance and value *now*. As we have come to see with all periods of art, what remains of interest to the future can never be assessed at the time it is being created, nor can it be seen with that in mind. Therefore, no judgements of the new art or any art can be based on either its current popularity or lack of it, and it is strange that some critics have attacked it on this score alone.

To attempt a justification of the New Super Realism, as some have done, on the grounds that the same thing was done by the Dutch realist Kitchen Painters or by Chardin in his still lifes, makes no sense when we remember that such painters were not obsessed with the common object as such, to the exclusion of everything else: they observed their objects within the context of an environment or setting and with a feeling for natural light and space, rendered in terms of personal brush-work. With the New Super Realism it has been noted that 'it is not the commonplace in a painting, but the commonplace *as* a painting.'

Such traditional qualities as design, layout, colour arrangement and form are not ignored in the new art; if anything they are over-stressed. But the difference between this sort of realism and that of the past is that the artist now sees his objects detached, separated from their immediate surroundings, things for and by themselves, as totemic symbols. A slavish desire to reproduce objects almost exactly as they are found, with the least possible amount of art intervention, has made the artist disregard the time-honoured Renaissance principles of naturalism, space, perspective and modelling. Instead he quotes an already art-rendered object, often in terms of the style in which it has been rendered. The virtuoso display of hand-painting is usually dismissed as unnecessary. There is, moreover, often no feeling whatsoever for the object, which is merely stated as a visual fact without any additions or subtractions.

Since many of the younger generation feel that all the battles of modern art have been fought and won by their elders, they seem determined to have fun with their art – to play with it and even to make jokes about it. Like the Surrealists before them, they rely to a large degree on humour for startling effect – but it is a mid-twentieth century brand of twisted or ironic humour called 'Camp'. A sort of stylish form of wit, accepted and exchanged by in-groups, this mode of expression has been taken up in a pseudo-fashion by the world of advertising and glossies, which treat seriously what is surely meant to be done light-heartedly and with tongue in cheek.

Such taste sports a humorous and constantly changing evaluation of things *passé* or out of style just before they come back into fashion (in the 'fifties, Art Nouveau was 'Camp', and in the 'sixties, 'World's Fair '39' is). In the New Super Realism, the taste of the immediate past, not quite datable and yet not quite out of sight, often comes in for re-evaluation: the 'forties pin-up girls, the cars of the 'fifties, post-war interior decoration, are all handled as items just out of reach which still have not yet found their place in history.

As defined by Susan Sontag, Camp is a 'mode of enjoyment, of appreciation – not judgement. Camp is generous, it wants to enjoy. It only *seems* like malice, cynicism . . . it relishes rather than judges . . .'

This is an extremely good description of some aspects of the New Super Realism in which Camp is expressed by a love of things being what they are not; by a fascination for the androgynous, particularly in over-exaggerated sexual forms which themselves become parodies; by ambiguity, irony, paradox and inverse humour; and by a feeling for artifice, for surface appeal, for thrilling, timely, sensational, stylish anti-conventions. Both the Low Camp of transvestism and the High Camp of exaggerated impersonation have a place here. Furthermore, the confusion of male and female, of reality with make-believe, of seriousness with fun, dignity with irreverence, etc., are important hallmarks of the new art, which appears to aim at being what Miss Sontag calls 'a solvent of morality', through a sponsorship of playfulness. To see this side of the New Super Realism gives it a further dimension and clarifies its desire to make fun of and have fun with what is at hand.

This fun aspect ties in with the Pop artist's lack of self-consciousness in using such impersonal techniques as silk-screening, air-brush spraying, stencilling, photographic montage and negative reproduction. Such commercial processes might of necessity remove the artist so far from the act of creation that he is no longer making what is ordinarily considered a work of art but merely arranging a piece of decorative display, as if he were an art-director. But these artists refuse to admit so limited a point of view, although they welcome the restrictions inherent in the processes themselves, and claim that if it is *accepted* as art, then it *is* art, no matter how closely it might resemble its manufactured model. And the public appears willing to consent, since many discussions about Pop Art have dealt with its merit, interest and importance, but few have questioned it as accepted art. With one brilliant stroke of irony the New Super Realists have swept away all the age-old and arbitrary divisions between 'fine', 'applied' and 'manufactured' art. Such a feat might imply that in the current situation where no established values exist, where the art-object is at the mercy of competitive museum patronage, big business, the hard-sell, celebrity promotion and a society that lives by what Harold Rosenberg calls 'the tradition of the new', only a sense of the inapposite can presumably reveal what is meaningful.

But perhaps the most important break-through accomplished by the New Super Realists is returning once more to the much denigrated act of looking at the real world. In dealing with 'reality', however, or at least with recognizable images, the new art throws open another vital question: what exactly is realism in art as compared to reality in life? The nineteenth-century *Salon* painter and Academician believed realism to be the development of illusionistic art techniques from the Renaissance onward; the Pre-Raphaelite believed it to be truth to nature observed minutely. The New Super Realist sets up an ambiguous situation with his realistic images. He does not make them into something else, as the Assemblage Artist does, nor are they excuses for flights of fantasy into the world of the sub-conscious as with the Surrealists. Instead, he quotes them accurately, as they appear, and at the same time creates a new reference for them by taking them out of a recognizable or accepted frame of understanding. As a result, we have ambivalent feelings towards recognizing a readable image and yet seeing it in terms of pure art. We can relate it only to itself, or return it to the real world where it came from, which means taking it away from art; it becomes neither one thing nor the other but two things at once.

Quotations in art go back to the Romans who rendered the Greeks, and there is nothing original in art's copying art. What is unique in this situation is that the original object itself is so art-less that it becomes confounded with its own 'artistic' image, and vice versa. They are like the six characters in search of their author; we do not know whether they are acting in a play or really existing.

This becomes a highly sophisticated piece of gamesmanship, particularly when some artists take the recognizable image and, by removing it so far from its own reality, turn it into an abstraction. If we can look at a comic strip or a blown up plaster hamburger as the lowest common denominator of illustration transposed into art by aesthetic adjustments, and then read it back as an abstraction, the entire argument of abstract versus representational, which has raged for half a century, becomes totally meaningless.

In returning to representation and illusion once more, the Pop-ists are neither trying to make a pure imitation of their objects indistinguishable from the original (as Life magazine points out, 'Everyone *knows* that's not art') nor are they aiming at an imaginative reconstruction of reality such as some nineteenth century academic painters sought. *Faute de mieux*, they are thrusting into a place somewhere between the two ideas, where the 'game of illusion' is used to cast us back into reality, without releasing us from the world of art.

Through dealing directly with reality in illusionism, the New Super Realists have taken a special interest in the photograph. Realist painting has come up against comparison with the photograph ever since 1839, when Delaroche remarked upon seeing the first daguerreotype: 'From today painting is dead'. But artists searching out reality in life through art, from the Pre-Raphaelites to the Pop-ists, have not accepted this; no one who has ever looked at a photograph and knows how to look at a painting could think that one would ever take the place of the other. However, the photograph can be and has been used by artists: Degas studied photographs to work out certain spatial problems; Corot studied light and atmospheric effects through them; Alma Tadema used them as architectural notations of a superior accuracy; Sickert copied them, perhaps out of perverseness. The New Super Realists do not use the photograph as a means of elevating popular taste to a higher artistic level by reproducing the familiar and the understood. They welcome the photograph as another visual source of found images, in an age of mass printing and reproduction. They see it, like television and the movies, as a visual stimulus which has sunk so deeply into our consciousness that we take it for granted; they feel it must be redefined for and by itself as both object and mechanical describer. By using the silk-screening or enlarging process, they can 'paint' their photographs on to

RICHARD SMITH: PHILIP MORRIS, 1964. *Silk screen print for the I.C.A., 19″ × 30″. Courtesy Institute of Contemporary Art, London.*

23

ALLEN JONES: FEMALE MEDAL, 1964.
Oil on canvas, 88" × 30". Courtesy Richard Feigen Gallery, New York.

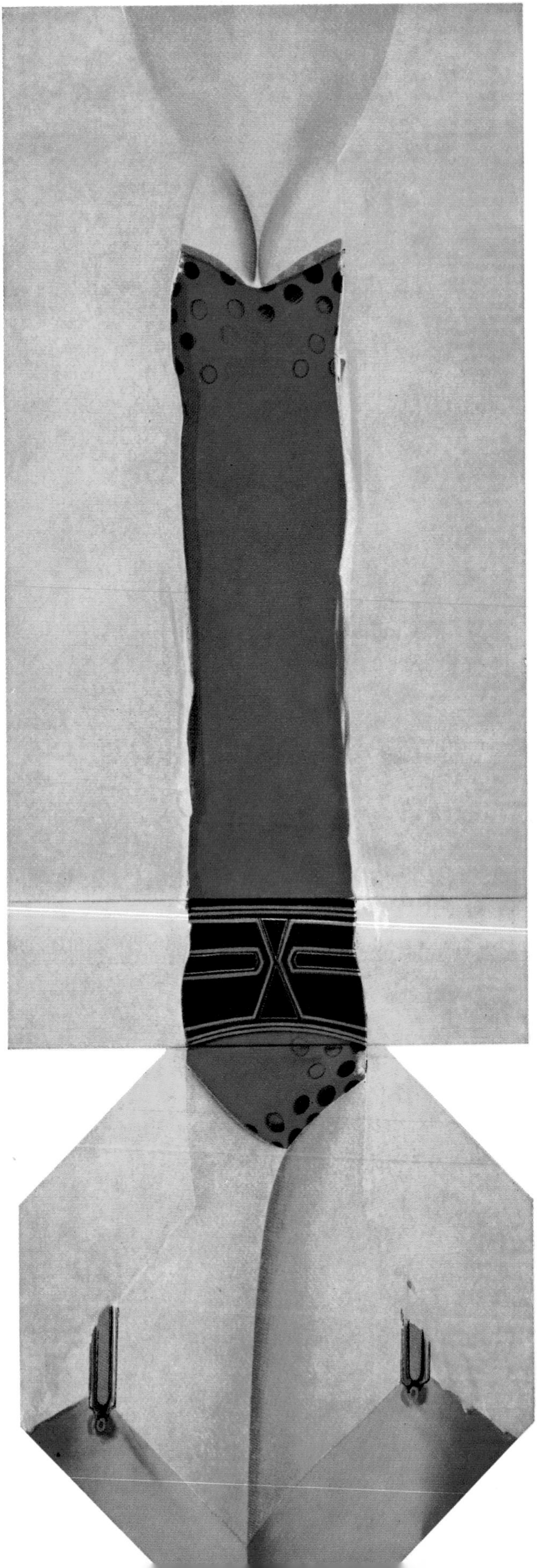

→

←

JOE TILSON: ZIGGURAT II, 1964.
*Paint on wood, 60" × 48".
Courtesy Marlborough-New London Gallery, London.*

CLAES OLDENBURG: HAMBURGER WITH PICKLE, PIECE OF
LAYER CAKE WITH ICING, AND GIANT ICE-CREAM CONE,
1962. *Green Gallery Exhibition in various media, room size.*

canvas; but, as the ultimate factual description of a reality which we take for granted as records of life in our daily paper, the photograph in their hands mysteriously loses all significance as a describer and becomes a means to pure design.

The investigation of the new nature of reality in both art and life, as well as the imagined 'gap' between the two, is a sort of *leit-motif* that runs through the whole group of New Super Realists, and has spread from painters and object-makers, into the world of literature, through Robbe-Grillet and Sarraute, into Post-Beat poetry, and to films through Truffaut, Antonioni and Resnais. Even 'Romantic' film-makers such as Gregory Markopoulos have consciously used certain commercial *clichés* in their works (in a film of the legends of Prometheus, Markopoulos used background paintings by Andy Warhol, against which the artist rode on a stationary reducing-cycle over a sea of cellophane).

Antonioni, however, is the best example of a romanticisation of the changed attitude toward life, and his film *Red Desert* appears as a manifesto to the new mechanised culture to which he feels we all must eventually adjust. He says, 'My intention . . . was to express the beauty of this world where even the factories and their chimneys are perhaps more beautiful than a line of trees, of which the eye has already seen too much. It is a rich world, lively, useful. For me, I try to say that the sort of neuroticism which one sees in the *Red Desert* is entirely a question of adaptability . . .' But more specifically, it has extended itself directly from artists such as Andy Warhol, who makes his own films, and Claes Oldenburg, whose 'Happenings' have been filmed numerous times, to Jack Smith's Camp masterpiece *Flaming Creatures* and Kenneth Anger's Pop fantasy, *Scorpio Rising*. In the theatre, the breakdown between audience and conventional stage-craft, through intensified and magnified actuality, has been achieved by Jack Gelber's *The Connection*, John Antrobus' *You'll Come to Love Your Sperm Test* and Le Roi Jones's *The Toilet*. Each of them scrutinises the object with a sharpened eye that tries to find between imitation and the new reality a sort of art. Such works record their objects, whether people *or* things, in a matter-of-fact way, without comment or feeling, yet give a new emotional meaning by accepting them completely and relentlessly.

An awareness of time is one of the elements most evident in the New Super Realism. Time is expressed in a variety of ways: as boredom, change, repetition, inconsequential sequence, movement, waiting. Rendering the timely into timelessness and vice versa, the new artists do not paint with eternity in mind, but with the moment at hand; moreover, they are not painting for, so much as about, the now.

As a member of a generation that grew up under the enormous influence of Abstract Expressionism, the New Super Realist has understood the temporal aspect of art.

27

The Abstract Expressionist, in seeking the eternal through the immediate 'gesture' of a spontaneous, expressive calligraphy, drove home to the younger generation just how temporal art can be; and such hard-won points cannot be dismissed from an artist's sensibility by merely returning art to time-respected realism.

The artist today is aware that time for us is no longer cyclical or repetitive, but makes life itself a constantly changing factor. The one element that continuously alters its shape visibly through time is life. Society is determined at present to live life through passing time, although, as J. B. Priestley observes in *Man and Time*, we try to disguise the fact in our obsessive emphasis on youth and mechanical invention. He believes that our present concepts of time have not only robbed us of the illusion of free will, but have placed us in an imaginary prison of our own construction. The New Super Realist seems to agree with Priestley by reflecting some of the ways we pass time: through mindless distraction, repetition, and an inexorable desire for change.

One way the new art deals with time is by exaggerating the impermanence of art in time, by using materials which are more than usually fragile and self-demolishing, or conversely by using materials which science and industry advertise as 'indestructible'. Another way of dealing with time was expressed earlier by some of the Pop-ists through the 'Happening'. Realising that art can sometimes be temporal and at other times spatial, the Happening attempted to combine both aspects at once. Apart from dealing with the space-distance between audience and artist, it destroyed the time lapse between creation and reception, by making art happen as the spectator watched or became actively involved. Here was another way to defy the art experience as a time-preserved occurrence, and Pop-ists such as Claes Oldenburg who used the Happening as a means of expression obviously developed much of their later art from this aesthetic. Another effort is made to come to grips with time by confounding objects of reality with their images as quoted in pre-existing commercial art forms, for a sensed time-lapse is necessary in a work to 'see' the artifice and compare it mentally with its real counterpart. In their use of the photograph, the most 'timely' visual document, the topical references lose their immediacy through repetition or juxtaposition and become a timeless blur.

The New Super Realists also come to grips with time by consciously changing styles as often as possible, and by working in several styles at once. To them, the concept of an evolutionary or 'progressive' art, such as we have been taught to believe has existed from Manet to Abstraction, and which we have come to expect, has little or no meaning. There is no progression in this art; instead it moves back and forth at will and at whim, as life does, without the imposition of a time concept;

as a result the works might be said to exist, without any sense of 'development'. It is interesting to note that of the many attacks on the new art by 'metaphysical' critics, the strongest and most often repeated has been that 'it won't live', that it is already 'old fashioned', 'out of date', 'over': all descriptions dealing with time.

Do all these renewed questions of philosophical concepts dealing with art, reality and life as seen and felt in terms of time and content, mean the end of the Renaissance? Already the hand-painted picture is declared dead, the shaped canvas says that a work of art has no pre-conceived form, while the Happening and the Environment signal the extension of art into life itself. And the New Super Realist claims that no subject or object, no matter how lowly or despised, is excluded from being dealt with by the artist in any way he chooses.

In an article entitled 'The end of the Renaissance?', Leonard B. Meyer has discussed at length the meanings of such new forms in art, to which the Pop-ists appear to be committed. Meyer says the new forms in music and painting tend to have no points of culmination such as one finds in so-called 'goal-oriented' art. Such art 'arouses no expectations, except presumably that it will stop. It is neither surprising, nor once you get used to it . . . is it particularly startling. It is simply *there*'. It does not have a beginning, middle and end as art of the past had, and does not move directionally from one point to another. Such an 'anti-teleological' art insists that our relationship to it, like our relationship to nature, ought to be one of total acceptance. 'The artist should accept the unanticipated result without seeking to impose his personal will on the materials or making them conform to some syntactical preconception of what ought to take place'. Similarly, we, as audience, are asked to entertain no preconceptions, make no predictions and force no organisation on the sounds, colours or words.

And with one fell swoop humanism as well as metaphysics is knocked to the ground. The new position, says Meyer, is one of 'uncompromising positivism'; or, to give it a better name, of 'Radical Empiricism.' Such Radical Empiricism has certainly been supported by the New Super Realists in their refusal to deny the aesthetic possibilities inherent in any pre-existing commercial art form.

Many of Meyer's theories are based on John Cage's sounds, and it must be remembered that Cage was a strong influence on both Robert Rauschenberg and Jasper Johns, each of whom in turn has been the emotional and intellectual force behind the New Super Realists. Cage wrote in his book *Silence* that '[The composer] must set about discovering a means to let sounds be themselves rather than vehicles for man-made theories or expressions of human sentiment'. He goes further and insists that 'art should be an affirmation of life – not an attempt to bring order out of chaos nor to suggest improvements in creation, but simply a way of waking up to the very life we are living, which is so excellent, once one gets one's mind and one's desires out of the way and lets it act of its own accord'. It is ideas like this that provide a backdrop against which the New Super Realist functions.

Meyer's Radical Empiricism demands that no event follows another, but simply 'comes after'. And, 'For the Radical Empiricist, the isolated object freshly experienced is the chief source of value'. Again, the audience is asked not to attempt to choose, even unconsciously, among alternative possibilities for continuation, since rational choice is a 'senseless fiction' in terms of such works. We are asked to remain detached, seeing, hearing and observing (and presumably enjoying) the objective occurences of empirical events.

In conclusion, Meyer informs us that the Radical Empiricist (and the Pop-ist) maintains a 'denial of the reality of relationships and the relevance of purpose, the belief that only individual sensations and not the connections between them are real, and the assertion that predictions and goals depend not on order existing in nature, but upon the accumulated habits and preconceptions of man'.

Thus, once more the relationship of cause and effect is considered only an illusion created by the mind through the channel of repetitive experience. This is upheld not only by John Cage's sounds, but by Rauschenberg's free associations in his assemblages, and by the New Super Realists in their supposedly arbitrary choice of subjects and objects, and by their total toleration of the banal.

What better age than this to re-state the non-existence of cause and effect when our scientists themselves tell us the latest discoveries have opened up so many possibilities of random choice in the universe that anything is likely, and that rational sequence can no longer be considered a certainty? Henry Margenau in *The Philosophy of Science*, himself admits that 'Physics knows . . . no plausible way of defining cause and effect.' It is interesting to see that physicists have now discovered a point that philosophers such as Hume hinted at two hundred years ago.

II   Beginnings in England

How did the New Super Realist get to these deep philosophical waters and is he
aware of such implications made by his art? Certainly Pop Art, as Lawrence Alloway
christened it, did not begin with any high-minded theories. Quite the contrary: in
England, where it, first crystallised into a group of artists with a shared point of
view, it was a vehicle of social protest and comment if anything.
Early in 1952, as Jasia Reichardt has chronicled it, a group of young London artists,
writers and architects formed a discussion group which met at the Institute of
Contemporary Arts. Determined to catch a sense of history as it was happening
rather than as it might one day be written, they called themselves the Independent
Group and met to discuss topics as wide-ranging as science, cybernetics, information
theory, philosophy, communications, mass media, pop music, fashion, industrial
design, violence in the cinema, and automobile styling. The Group included Eduardo
Paolozzi, William Turnbull, Richard Hamilton, Peter Reyner Banham, Lawrence
Alloway, Sandy Wilson, Nigel Henderson, Alison and Peter Smithson, John Joelcker
and John McHale among others.
The Group formed the hard core of advanced thinking at that time which saw the
paradox of the creative individual in a mass-think society that grew stranger
and more complicated daily. It was at a meeting in 1952 that Eduardo Paolozzi
dealt directly with Pop imagery by projecting on a screen for his delighted audience
a series of 'found' images made up mostly of advertising material. Such matter itself
was not all that different from what Kurt Schwitters might have used, but when
Paolozzi enlarged his objects by means of the projection screen, they took on a new,
mysterious and unfamiliar quality through their isolation and blown-up scale. The
following year, another event was arranged, this time as a joint effort between
Paolozzi and Peter Smithson; it was called 'Parallel of Life and Art'.
Preoccupation with the popular culture directed the Group's discussions, according

to Miss Reichardt, and evenings would be spent talking seriously about Westerns or Science Fiction and other forms of popular art. She admits that: 'The very notion of culture (through the discussions) changed before one's eyes . . . the unlimited communication assailing one in the form of radio, television, reading matter, had forced its way into one's consciousness and could not be ignored.'

But apparently the real inspiration and insight into 'popular culture' was provided by a trunkful of glossy American magazines which John McHale brought back to England in 1955 from a trip to the U.S. *Esquire*, *Mad*, *Playboy* and other slick publications brought a whole new conception of Pop to the Group, and America was looked to 'as the source of a new and unexpected inspiration, as a romantic land with an up-to-date culture, a hot-bed of new sensibility in art'. If before the war America had traditionally turned to Europe for a lead in art, Europe, or at least a group of artists in London, began to see the New World romantically, as the take-off point into 'tomorrow'.

Richard Hamilton was most strongly influenced by these factors, and in 1956 at the Whitechapel Gallery exhibition in London called 'This is Tomorrow', he created the first genuine work of Pop, and certainly one of the earliest fully-matured pieces of New Super Realism called *Just What is it that Makes Today's Homes so Different, so Appealing?* The picture contained not only a grotesquely over-developed *Physique Pictorial* hero, but a nude stripper, with her breast tips coyly covered by sequined decorations. Photo montages described the home in which they lived as containing a large 'painting' on the wall taken directly from a comic book called 'Young Romance', a tape recorder in the foreground, a television set in the background, and a lampshade with a Ford motor-car's coat of arms emblazoned across it. Through the window in the distance one could see that *The Al Jolson Story* was playing twice daily at the local cinema. The muscle-man carried in his right hand a large lollipop called 'Tootsie' with the word 'Pop' exaggerated.

The exhibition, which had twelve sections, was designed to draw the spectator into the works as an 'Environment'. Hamilton's section (apart from *Just what is it . . .*, which was done as an entrance display) was worked out in conjunction with John McHale and the architect John Joelcker. It contained a huge blow up of 'Robbie the Robot', 16-feet high and complete with flashing eyes and teeth, looking like a cross between a cartoon fantasy and a Paolozzi sculpture. In fact, it was a piece of cinema publicity material borrowed from the London Pavilion in Piccadilly Circus. The robot carried an unconscious girl who was clothed in a skin-tight tunic. Superimposed was a movie still of Marilyn Monroe in her most famous scene from *The Seven Year Itch* with skirts blowing high. This was the first time

Marilyn, who later became the high priestess of Pop imagery, appeared in the New Super Realism.

The Whitechapel event was not new to London. All this had been seen in 1954 in a totally different form. Perhaps the first successful Environment work in Europe was an exhibition of the Diaghilev Ballet presented by Richard Buckle at Forbes House where the spectator moved through the series of decors which were designed with the help of stage-craft, music and smells, to incorporate him in the displays and to make him a physical part of what he was seeing. And significantly, it was the Diaghilev Exhibition that first gave John Cage the opportunity to set up four pianos in different rooms wired for sound, which projected 'noises' throughout the house as spectators wandered about the exhibition. But the Whitechapel show differed in so far as it was not so much concerned with evoking a period charm, as aiming, through the collaboration of artist, architect and sculptor, at a new awareness of present day life and its surroundings by extending art so that it was something in which the spectator could actively involve himself.

Hamilton's definitions of Pop had by this time grown to include the material that the artist used as a source of fine art, which came out of the popular culture. And although Alloway had thought up the expression in 1954, he still confined it strictly to the popular culture objects which had little or no fine art merit. It was not until 1962, when Pop was snowballing into an international craze, that Alloway enlarged his definition to include the fine art products that the new group of artists in London and New York were producing.

In the catalogue of the Whitechapel show, Hamilton wrote: 'We reject the notion that tomorrow can be expressed through the formal presentation of rigid formal concepts. Tomorrow can only extend the range of the present body of visual experience. What is needed is not a definition of meaningful imagery but the development of our perceptive potentialities to accept and utilise the continual enrichment of visual material.'

In the following year (1957) he committed to paper exactly what Pop Art was to him as an artist: popular (designed for a mass audience); transient (short-term solution); expendable (easily forgotten); low-cost; mass-produced; young (aimed at youth); witty; sexy; gimmicky; glamorous; and, last but not least, Big Business.

How influential Hamilton was on the new generation of painters that emerged in the 1961 annual Young Contemporaries exhibition is difficult to determine. But he was known and admired by Peter Blake and Richard Smith, both of whom were at the Royal College of Art from 1953 to 1956/7. These two artists, who at one time shared a studio, might be considered a link between Hamilton's generation and the group of younger artists who were to study at the Royal College of Art from 1959 to 1962.

Certainly Hamilton's work was known at the Whitechapel Art Gallery and at the I.C.A., both feeding grounds for budding young artists, but his output was spread thinly over a long period (his recent exhibition of thirty-five works represented nearly the total production of eight years) and he himself admits that very little of his work was seen in England. Thus, his position in British Pop is perhaps one of a spiritual force, rather than of a father figure as Blake's or Smith's would appear to be, and as such he has little direct relationship with the younger New Super Realists, although he is definitely a Pop artist.

Paolozzi, from Scotland, also contributed to 'This is Tomorrow'. With the Smithsons he arranged an aluminium patio, which was striking for its machine-made toughness. He has earned much admiration from the younger artists in London but, although of the same generation as American Robert Rauschenberg, he has not been anything like as influential. His cast 'sculptures', reminiscent of slot machines, fairground machinery and IBM equipment are somehow too monolithic and removed from the original, too elusively suggestive to be called New Super Realist. However, he had been doing 'targets' as far back as 1948, which may or may not have been seen by American Jasper Johns who used the target symbol as one of the first recognizable objects in his Abstract Expressionist canvases of 1955. Unlike Johns, Paolozzi's targets are less hard-hitting and relentless and more romantically nostalgic, with their oblique references to fun-fair surroundings and games of chance. A sly comment on who was first with the target was made in 1961 by Peter Blake, when he produced his own target and labelled it *The First Real Target?* on the canvas itself. (Here was a sublime piece of pure painting about painting).

Blake, who left the Royal College of Art in 1956, had a one-man show at the I.C.A. in London in 1960, and his works of the preceding two years created much interest in the younger generation. He had studied popular art for some years, and his interest in popular culture has a studious air about it, mixed up with nostalgic reminiscences of the recent and distant past. It often sports a strong literary content, in the tradition of English art, and in the 1964 Shakespeare Exhibition he proved himself to be a history painter on a grand scale and in the grand manner. But stylistically he meant little to the younger group of David Hockney, Derek Boshier, Allen Jones and Peter Phillips.

Another earlier student of the Royal College of Art who was to mean much to the young New Super Realists was Richard Smith. He left the R.C.A. in 1957 and two years later went to New York, where he remained during the whole

RICHARD HAMILTON: JUST WHAT IS IT THAT MAKES TODAY'S
HOMES SO DIFFERENT, SO APPEALING?, 1956. *Collage,*
10¼ × 9¾". Collection Mr Edwin Janss, Jr., California.

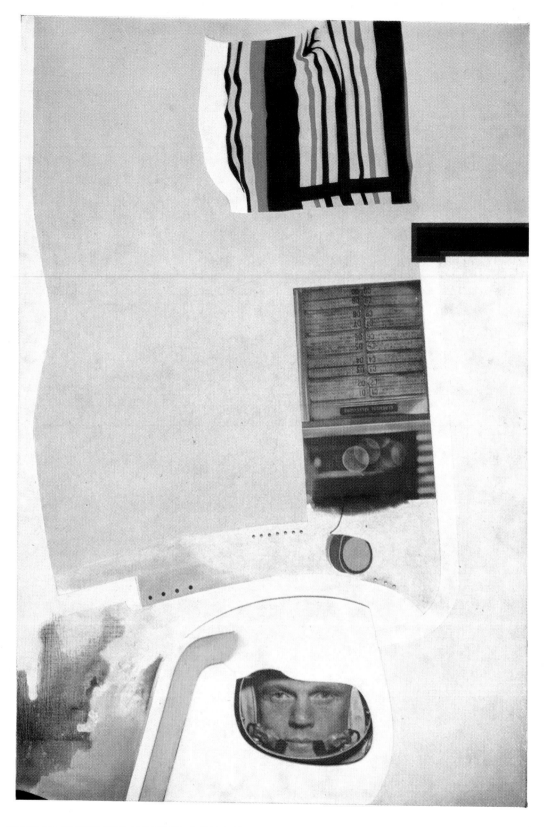

RICHARD HAMILTON: TOWARDS A DEFINITIVE STATEMENT ON THE COMING TRENDS IN MEN'S WEAR AND ACCESSORIES (D), 1963. *Gouache, metal foil and collage, 48" × 32". Courtesy Hanover Galblery, London.*

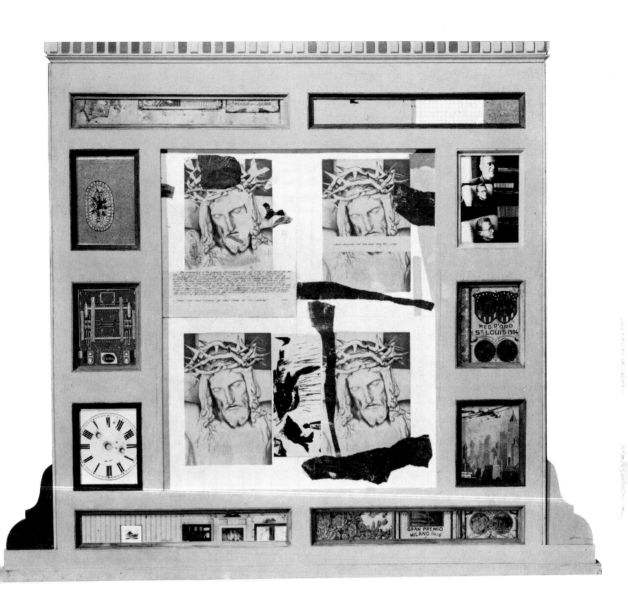

EDUARDO PAOLOZZI AND R. B. KITAJ: WORK IN PROGRESS 21,
1962. Various materials on wood, 34″ × 32½″.
Collection Mrs G. Keiller.

ROBERT RAUSCHENBERG: BUFFALO II, 1964. *Oil on canvas, 8' × 6'. Collection Mr Robert Mayer.*

gestation of the new generation. When he returned in 1961, he brought with him an entire attitude to painting which was strictly American and which he had learned in New York from the generation of Jasper Johns and others. His freedom with paint, his refusal to admit traditional limitations in shape, and his sense of scale greatly impressed artists such as Boshier and Phillips. Boshier, in particular, a close friend, quickly changed his direction from strict Pop Art to a sort of 'Pop Op' or geometrical-shaped canvas painting under the influence of Smith. As Smith himself explains it: 'I set myself the task of mingling commercial atmosphere with abstract art'. His own pop emblems and symbols, taken from commercial packaging, have been so transformed as to bring his work into a wholly different sphere of New Super Realism and then out again into more varied extensions of Abstract Expressionists and Hard-Edge art. His experiments with shaping canvases has brought him beyond the self-limitations of popular subject matter, and he was most instrumental in releasing much British Pop from a tight, restricted attitude.

The same is true of David Hockney, whose early works of 1960 and 1961, contained literal references to packaging (his *Typhoo Tea* picture has now become almost legendary). Although he still takes much of his material out of physical culture magazines and glossy publications, his style has become extremely personal and idiosyncratic. He has affected a naive approach to drawing and handling of paint, which does not belie a fine technical craftmanship and a shrewd, sophisticated sense of irony; his images have become removed from their prototypes through his consciously artless intervention.

The Young Contemporaries exhibition of 1961 not only brought the London Pop-ists to public attention, but it presented for the first time the work of R. B. Kitaj, an older student of the Royal College. Kitaj is an American who arrived in London in 1958; his fellow students were Jones, Hockney, Boshier and Phillips, and much has been made of his influence on them. A first hand knowledge of American techniques and attitudes to painting, a certain breadth of style, and an interest in commercial methods made him an important source of information to the British.

Two other English 'Pop-ists' who have caused much attention are Joe Tilson and Anthony Donaldson. Tilson is perhaps the better known, since he appeared in the British Pavilion at the 1964 Venice Biennale. His work employs carpentered wood shapes, sometimes painted, and invariably constructed. The subject matter includes symbols and lettering – often they are shapes with literal references. For instance, he will construct a giant open key-hole and then attach the word KEY to the bottom, or he will put together a large blow-up of an eye in horn-rimmed spectacles and call it LOOK in bold letters under the image. His work lacks subtlety but the craftmanship is first-rate, and the images are very strong.

Like the Americans, Anthony Donaldson 'has made nonsense of the figurative abstract controversy', as David Thompson puts it. The fact that he uses the *clichés* of Pop imagery, such as strippers, racing cars, pin-ups, etc. is almost unimportant: he is clearly concerned first and foremost with making an abstract pattern, and the use of such subject matter appears incidental. He prefers the kaleidoscopic fragmentation of images, or the repeated slicing of the image as it might perhaps be seen on a badly adjusted television screen or in a series of cinema film frames. Repeats of the same image fascinate him, more for the interesting compositional effect than from any desire to show an oppressive accumulation of matter, as in the case of Andy Warhol. Painting in a flat, hard-edge style, he confines his colours to pastel baby pinks and sky blues, with which we have always associated a kind of sentimental surburban horror. Like other Pop-ists he wants an impersonal finish, free from any painterly stylisation, and he works from photographs, transferring his design by means of tracing and stencilling.

The entire school of New Super Realism in London differs as radically from the American school as in a former generation the American Cubists differed from their French counterparts. In London there is the same interest in Pop subjects: targets, pin-ups, motorcycles, cars, sex, the space age, newspapers, photography and advertising. But there is a sort of unspoken acknowledgement that New York is the fountainhead of popular culture (with the exception of the Beatles) and London is incapable of competing with it. What results is a sort of playing with Pop in the hands of the clever, rather than a tough coming to grips with it; a European sensibility is retained at all costs; craftmanship is respected, and new-found idioms are never pushed to the breaking point. Everything is treated affectionately, and with a sense of style and fun.

The New Super Realism in British painting somehow seems more honest and forthright an expression than that of the previous generation of Abstract Expressionists who tried to shape a style on the American model-plan. The young urban artists' work is a far cry also from the manicured constructivism of Victor Pasmore and Ben Nicholson, and from the sado-masochistic horror-work of Francis Bacon. Even Sutherland's Frenchified colours and forms have not counted for much. The young artists have sprung up with a flamboyance and self-confidence that fits oddly into the traditional pattern of British painting.

Such a new kind of British artist was perhaps envisaged by Virginia Woolf when she wrote of D. H. Lawrence: 'One feels that he echoes nobody, continues

no tradition, is unaware of the past, of the present save as it affects the future.'
Unlike the Americans, most Londoners, apart from Hamilton, had no historical reverence for Marcel Duchamp until the Tate exhibition of 1966, nor are they necessarily determined to work within a certain recognized language created by Dada; and they are less determined to reinstate obtrusive non-art objects as aesthetic forms. They have worked towards releasing themselves from the tyranny of the rectangle, and they delight in shaping their canvases to suit their compositions. Although their forms, colours and designs depend on advertising illustration, they steer from the absolutely hideous and the relentlessly ugly, to some middle course where the raucous and vulgar take on a colourful dazzle and jazzy brilliance.

This new approach (and the Londoners have mostly been painters rather than object-makers) has brought a surprisingly vital and exciting element into British art. It is as if the British, relinquishing the chores of an empire, had once more returned to the fireside passion of artistically investigating modes of life and changes in environment. There is a lack of direct involvement in this, but then, after all, Londoners can never be New Yorkers, no matter how mechanised their city life becomes, and the British themselves are too fond of eccentricity, wit and self-reflection to entirely embrace the mass-think culture.

As in the eighteenth century, when Englishmen toured Italy in search of classical art – then considered the commonly shared culture of the time – so today the English artist does the Grand Tour in America, seeking out the contemporary American popular culture. Most of the English have either been in America for extended visits or else divide their time between the two countries; their purpose in this is not to ape U.S. art, but to experience at first hand the common cultural *milieu* that promises soon to encircle the entire western world.

After Richard Smith broke ground in New York with his first one-man exhibition in 1961, most of the new generation of British artists followed his example with long stays in New York. Although they have regarded New York as their art Mecca, much as a pre-war generation treated Paris, they have still maintained their own individuality. Perhaps only Richard Smith has been influenced so deeply by long visits to New York that he paints more like a New Yorker than a Londoner; but even here there is still something British about his sensitivity to tone and line that continues to mark him nationally. On the whole, the new British artists in the pop vernacular have solidified and strengthened their work considerably through their direct contact with New York painting, without basically changing character.

British artists retain a strong literary streak, and their love of play, whimsy, and pun is central enough to keep them from making heavy weather of their chosen subjects. A gay, off-handed, pleasure-loving breed, they do not feel bound to stick so closely to their models and sources as Americans do; instead, they consciously play the game of 'artist' and rearrange, reassort, juxtapose and fragment images, determined to come between the ready-made or re-found original and its translation into art.

One thing is clear. The British New Super Realists have had absolutely no influence on the Americans and, apart from a certain canny adaptation of technical tricks and a freedom with scale, they are determined that the Americans will have little influence on them. That they insist on retaining their own peculiar sensibilities is a healthy sign. In an easy, natural and unaffected return to 'realism', always a style so close to the core of English painting, these artists have succeeded on their own terms, without any of the former inferiority complex that British art was wont to suffer under the French hegemony.

This can sometimes be misinterpreted. David Sylvester, in a piece on Pop Art called 'Art in a Coke Climate' (in which he made a distinction between a 'Wine Culture' and 'Coke Culture'), set down what he felt were some essential differences between European and American Pop.

'It seems to me', he wrote, 'that the British artists by and large take a far more romantic and optimistic view of Coke Culture than the Americans do. If this is so, the reason would clearly be that Coke Culture has not yet completely taken Britain over and so exerts a more exotic fascination for us.'

He decided, in conclusion, that, 'Most of British Pop Art is a dream, a wistful dream of far-off Californian glamour as sensitive and tender as the Pre-Raphaelite dream of far-off medieval chivalry. I like it as I like Millais's *Ophelia* and Arthur Hughes's *The Long Engagement*.'

This is somewhat misleading, for whereas the Pre-Raphaelites attempted to escape the materialism which they feared and despised, either by turning to a supra-real or 'ideal' world of the story-book past, or by moralising grandly about the ills of the present, the New Super Realist embraces with awe, amazement and cynical acceptance the commercialism of the twentieth century.

On the other hand, the reference to academic *genre* painting is perceptive, since in some cases the accurate detailing, high finish and graduated modelling that the New Super Realists adopt from commercial models, have anachronistically been carried on into the mid-twentieth century by illusionistic advertising art techniques which have persisted through all the art revolutions of this century.

42

In America

In the complicated and fast-moving history of the New Super Realism as an international style, it has been generally believed that because the term Pop Art was invented in London, the movement (if one can call it that) has British roots. Apart from the fact that Mr. Alloway came to the Guggenheim Museum in 1962, with a more than liberal attitude towards what he called Pop, and lectured widely on the subject, there is little direct relationship between the two, except what England took straight from American culture.

A basic difference is the visual pressures of advertising and ad-mass communications in New York, which are greater on the artist there than they are in London. In a city with six commercial television channels operating round the clock in either black and white or colour, with six major daily newspapers carrying dozens of pages of advertising, with hundreds of glossies and cheap sex journals, with scores of movie houses (some open at eight in the morning, some open all night), with a town centre decorated with real giant-sized cigarette smoke rings blown over Times Square, with enlargements of movie stars thirty feet high, and with most blank walls covered with mammoth billboards, and until recently with a real waterfall on top of a building, the environment is bound to produce totally different reactions from artists who wish to exploit basic elements in the life of the city.

To understand the New Super Realism in New York is not only to understand the Pop culture which produced it, or the atmosphere of rampant commercialism which prevails, but to set the whole New York scene against its post-war mania for 'modern' art, and its emergence as the art capital of the Western world.

The Abstract Expressionist break-through by Americans who met and conquered their European counterparts was of the greatest importance, and this movement continues to be respected by the younger artists. It will never be forgotten that until the early 'fifties European art dominated and controlled U.S. painting and sculpture to a stifling degree: Pollock and Co. effected a change which meant more than an aesthetic revolution; it meant that at last the ignored American artist had earned a respectable place in his own society. Now, after Abstract Expressionism has fulfilled its central function, the New Super Realism has become an important contender for the second wholly American style of art to capture the imagination of European artists.

Interested critics have taken a strong, somewhat hysterical stand on the issue of so-called Pop Art, since the New Super Realists appear on the face of it to be kicking the whole of the American achievement out of the window. Slanderous attacks of Fascism, Nazism, homosexuality, and drug addiction rang in the air when it became evident around 1961 and 1962 that there was something solid, well-defined and committed about the new art. 'Metaphysical' writers such as Harold Rosenberg and Clement Greenberg who had staked their reputations on the continuation of Abstract Expressionism, took strong stands, and Peter Selz, presumably speaking on his own behalf rather than for the Museum of Modern Art where he worked, wrote emotional diatribes which now read as curious documents of an older, apparently less flexible age.

The younger critics and art historians, among them Henry Geldzahler, G. R. Swenson, Barbara Rose, Donald Judd and Robert Rosenblum, found themselves in the embarrassing position of defending a movement which was made to appear as if it were the 'enemy' of a previous movement. As for the artists themselves, their frank admission of a debt to their forebears did little to prevent their being assailed as cheap, meretricious, unworthy heirs of the 'heroic' years of American painting. Actually, their only crime was a return to figuration and the banal trivia of city life, in a desperate attempt to open up the possibilities of art from the narrow confines it had settled into at the hands of the Abstract Expressionists, who believed that only the act of painting itself could reveal value, individuality and genius. The younger artists merely wanted to do something different; they were not attempting to divorce themselves from what had happened before.

This is apparent when one notes how many New Super Realists in New York pay homage to Willem de Kooning. One of the greatest Abstract Expressionists of the post-war period, de Kooning was always something of a maverick to his contemporaries. For one thing he refused to relinquish his interest in the figure – particularly the female figure. That the younger generation found in him a source of inspiration, is made evident in G. R. Swenson's *Art News* interviews with eight Pop Artists. In his unpublished papers, Swenson records that Robert Rauschenberg's painting with the two real electric fans in it, later called *Pantomime*, was in some part initiated after a remark by de Kooning. Rauschenberg is reported as saying: 'De Kooning at that time kept talking about the different ways that paint dries, and that seemed to me an interesting thing to try to show in a painting, and that's one of the things I tried to do in that painting.' The two fans used 'to dry the paint' were installed; the artist hesitated to report the story in *Art News*, 'because Tom Hess [the editor] thinks that everything I do comes from de Kooning.'

In his monograph on de Kooning, Thomas B. Hess has revealed that the artist's subject matter often has affinities to popular culture motifs: in describing his *Women* series, one of which, almost half Pop, was called *Marilyn*, 1954, he wrote: 'The artist has indicated, half jokingly, that his women are sisters to the giant ladies (girls?) that are pasted on mailtrucks and billboards – enormous public goddesses of droll sex and earnest sales pitches. He also has pointed out that the women are masked by the "American smile" – that ubiquitous, vacant, friendly, distant, polite expression (in one sketch for a woman her smile was cut out of a "T Zone" ad for Camels in *Life* magazine).' The same T-Zone symbol was to appear later in James Rosenquist's work.*

Tom Wesselmann, in Swenson's interviews, said, 'De Kooning gave me my content and motivation. My works evolve from that.' And Jasper Johns – along with Rauschenberg one of the major influences on the New Super Realists – said that his two beer cans came indirectly from a suggestion by the older artist: 'De Kooning was annoyed with my dealer, Leo Castelli, for some reason, and said something like, "that son of a bitch; you could give him two beer cans and he could sell them". I heard this and thought, what a sculpture – two beer cans! It seemed to fit in perfectly with what I was doing, so I did them – and Leo sold them.'

Of course no Pop painting looks like a de Kooning; the point is that he provided an inspirational contact with the older generation that was in turn reformed and changed into a new attitude about painting. De Kooning himself is reported to have said that as far as the Pop Artists are concerned, 'I am on one mountain, and they are on another.'

Jim Dine says of his work, and of the new painting, 'I don't believe there was a sharp break and this is replacing Abstract Expressionism. I believe this is the natural course of things . . . I tie myself to Abstract Expressionism like fathers and sons.'

Only Robert Indiana appears to find that the new art 'springs newborn out of a boredom with the finality and over-saturation with Abstract Expressionism which, by its own aesthetic logic, *is* the END of art, the glorious pinnacle of the long pyramidal creative process.' He concludes that, 'stifled by this rarefied atmosphere some young painters turn back to some less exalted things like Coca Cola, ice

* The 'T-zone' is a 'T' square superimposed over the mouth and throat of a smoker of Camels to indicate the area of 'smoking pleasure'.

cream sodas, big hamburgers, super markets and "EAT" signs. They are eye hungry; they are pop . . .'

Objects made by such artists as Claes Oldenburg and George Segal have a roughened expressionist surface texture, and with Oldenburg there is a pure use of paint expressively, complete with drips and runs, although the colours themselves indicate the real objects to which they refer. With Dine, who combines ready-made objects with a pure expressionist paint surface, the brushwork, the style and the handling of materials come directly from action painting.

Allan Kaprow, who first began to give Happenings in 1957, based on earlier collages, says it was a 'total' experience at a Jackson Pollock exhibition, in which he stood entirely surrounded by Pollock's works, that gave him the idea for the first Environment work. Basing his plan on John Cage's *Theory of Inclusion*, he widened the range of materials, to include cloth, photos, mirrors, electric lights, plastic film, aluminium foil, rope, straw and various sounds and smells. These materials multiplied in number and density, extending away from the flat canvas surface until there was no longer a pictorial point of departure and the whole gallery became filled.

Moveable or moving parts began to suggest themselves and Kaprow admits: 'Roughly speaking, I had in mind the totality of most everyday environments where one takes an active part, and I used many of these as models; a subway station, penny arcade, forest, kitchen, etc., though not in any literary way.'

Another artist, George Segal, departed from this position with his extraordinary life-sized plaster-cast models of real people in full-scale interior settings (reminiscent, perhaps, of a shop-window display, framed in an imaginary glass-fronted rectangle); and Oldenburg created an entire show called *The Street* in 1960, together with Jim Dine's *The House*. Later he produced the first version of his *The Store*.

Working with Dine, Oldenburg founded the *Ray Gun* theatre in 1960 ('It's a name I imagined. Spelled backwards it sounds like New York and it's all sorts of things. It has mystic overtones'): and there with his wife and other members of the 'cast' he organized his Happenings. Three nights would be devoted to discussion, working out time, the objects and the spatial compositions. His major problem was to give his 'performers' free reign to some degree, controlling the action and character of the whole production. The events were never completely unplanned or lacking in sound or action. He never used a traditional audience, but an 'in-group' of thirty-five, crowded together with the performers into one whole. The results were 'messy, vulgar, and sometimes enchanting.'

Barbara Rose has cleverly remarked that Pop has a lot to do with Johns and Rauschenberg, but they have little to do with it. This is not entirely true. Rauschenberg

JASPER JOHNS: PAINTED BRONZE, 1960. *Cast bronze, painted,*
$5\frac{1}{2}'' \times 8'' \times 4\frac{3}{4}''$. *Collection Mr Robert C. Scull, New York.*

JIM DINE: RED ROBE, 1964. *Oil on canvas and collage, 84″ × 60″. Courtesy Sidney Janis Gallery,*
New York.   →

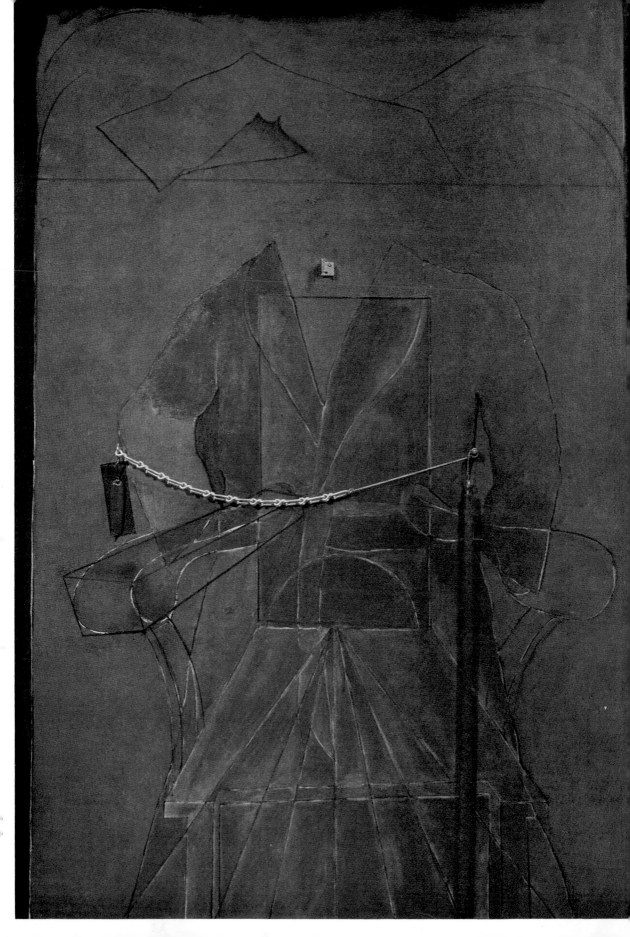

JAMES ROSENQUIST: SILVER SKIES, 1962. *Oil on canvas, 78" × 16½'. Collection Mr and Mrs Robert C. Scull, New York.*

TOM WESSELMANN: GREAT AMERICAN NUDE 51, 1963. *Oil on canvas, collage, 120" × 144". Courtesy Green Gallery, New York.*

for one, may be seen in terms of the New Super Realism much the way Picasso's work of 1912 to 1914 can be seen in terms of Dada. He was a forerunner, a strong influence, and his work continues to cross and re-cross constantly with the new painting. But he is so individually a 'performance' artist in the tradition of, say, Picasso, that he will never adhere to a thoroughly consistent point of view. His use of silk-screen processes, photographs of Kennedy, and a return to the flat canvas and rectangle, which he used almost as soon as he heard what Andy Warhol was doing, and perhaps even before he saw his work, brings him closer to the group; but his way of using photographic silk screening is so entirely personal, so fraught with free association and poetic juxtaposition, that he appears too romantic an artist to be considered Pop.

However, he was a great source of ideas to the young generation of the New York School. Round about 1955, now called the 'Crisis Year', various solutions were sought to break the absolute rule of Abstract Expressionism, and Rauschenberg's work was the first to appear as one answer to where art goes after abstraction. As has been noted before, John Cage was a key figure in helping to release both Johns and Rauschenberg from feelings of self-limitation and self-consciousness, and his example allowed them to consider a wider choice of materials and approach. As with Cage's 'sounds', anything and everything was possible through his *Theory of Inclusion*. It was in 1955 that Rauschenberg painted his first totally successful object-work, made out of a quilt and a pillow. Without money for canvas, and not needing his bed quilt, he put it on a stretcher. 'It looked strange without a pillow, so I added the pillow', he says, adding that it was not a preconceived idea. The entire surface was covered with a strongly expressionistic handling of paint and objects freely applied. Rauschenberg felt such 'combinations' of objects and paint demanded a new name, since they were neither painting nor sculpture, and he invented the term 'Combine'.

Rauschenberg's choice of sub-aesthetic objects, transformed into something else by being placed in a new painterly context, exercise a powerful effect. The objects, such as discarded chairs, stuffed sheep, clocks, radios and electric fans, are meant to lose their old identity and become an integral part of the work. Such an approach to ready-made objects or re-found cast-offs re-established the long lost contact between reality and art, which have become farther and farther divorced as painting has come to deal more with painting than with life. Rauschenberg crystallised the entire problem for himself and his generation with his now famous statement: 'Painting relates to both art and life. Neither can be made (I try to act in the gap between the two).' Both art and life were thus meant to be mutually enhancing,

DEREK BOSHIER: I WONDER WHAT MY HEROES THINK OF THE SPACE RACE, 1962. *Oil on canvas, 96″ × 69½″. Lords Gallery, London (Heroes represent Nelson, Lincoln and Buddy Holly).*

and both could and should enrich and complement each other.

Jasper Johns, on the other hand, arrived at similar problems at the same time, but in a totally different way. For one thing, he continued 'to paint about painting' despite his interest in real objects. Both he and Rauschenberg paradoxically studied at Black Mountain, North Carolina, with Josef Albers, the Bauhaus teacher and Optical painter, who now forgets them both. But clearly Johns learned much about optical illusionism and after-images from Albers, as is evident from his all-white Numbers painting and the barely visible Target images in his 'abstract' collages.

Unlike Rauschenberg, he usually works with a single object which is investigated both intellectually and sensuously, rather than with a number of objects dealt with emotionally. His work alludes to other painting styles and forms, and one feels one is meant to savour it as a connoisseur, rather than enjoy it passionately as a strong, full-bodied direct experience. In works by Rauschenberg, every drip and splatter in the gesture has its own life even if part of the whole, whereas in those of Johns it is the careful touch and manipulation that reveal the feeling, and these cannot be experienced except as part of the aesthetic *Gestalt* of the work. His purely Abstract Expressionist works, in which a stencilled word such as 'Tango' creeps into a corner of the picture, have a literary subtlety that Rauschenberg is not concerned with. Rauschenberg's apparently self-destructive surfaces, littered with junk and covered with smears, appear to be a way for him to overcome his own virtuosity; his conscious use of the ugly may be a means for him to defy a facile technique which could take over completely if he is not careful. This is born out by the *Dante* 'rubbings' and some of the silk screens, which have a tendency to become 'pretty' without the hideous and tough objects with which we must struggle. Johns, for his part, has an almost onanistic affection for his surfaces; he fondles them carefully, and titillates his materials until they reach a highly nervous level of sensibility.

Reputedly furious with the rows raging in New York between the Abstract Expressionists and the figurative artists, Johns set out in 1955 to paint a purely abstract work – in terms of a recognizable image. What resulted was the series of flags and targets. Taking two such commonly accepted and understood symbols, one national, the other universal, he created a pure expressionist skin of paint to sheathe his object/subject. The delicate build-up of collage surface in his *Green Target* covered with paint, mysteriously screens the symbol which appears to lurk, almost mystically, underneath it. With the flags, the spectator is faced with a problem of viewing something *exactly* as it is in reality, only in terms of sensitively worked surface of expressionist brush strokes. Such brush strokes would look tame in pure Abstract Expressionism but, used to depict a recognizable object, they look outrageous. By using such 'tangible' paint to create 'tangible' objects, Johns almost cancels out the objects themselves in the ambiguous nature of the work. Whereas Rauschenberg is coming to terms with objects considered totally sub-aesthetic, Alan Solomon feels that Johns is investigating the entire question of what 'taste' is, and its suitability in terms of objects never considered paintable before. Such objects could not be dealt with in the old Cubist manner, Solomon decides, because of 'the obtuse density and passivity' of the images which make the spectator ask why they have been painted and thus make him look more carefully and intensely than before. The fact of the banal image and the fact of pure painting are constantly balancing each other.

Some of the most beautiful works by Johns are his sculptures, which are either cast in bronze or made permanent with a coat of Sculpmetal, a commercial product that hardens into a metallic-like surface. Objects such as the twin Ballantine beer cans, one punched open and empty, the other unopened and minutely different in size (both cast in bronze and covered with 'painted' labels), invite the eye to compare the shapes with reality, and to notice the slightest variations between two cans mounted on the same plinth and the original which exists in memory. By such tricks of the eye, and by hand-painting the surface of his objects in a free way, Johns has reversed gear with the New Super Realism and is insisting that the commonplace and mass-produced can be made by the artist into something unique, and highly personal.

From this point it is easy to see how a rising generation of artists might be fascinated by the possibilities inherent in such a broadening of the art vocabulary. If such things can be taken from their commonplace idiom and effectively placed into art, then surely the whole universe of visual sensations and experiences to which our eyes have been closed might be opened once more to investigation. It is an easy jump from this to the next stage where a wealth of second-hand, ready-made, manufactured and mass-produced imagery might be dealt with aesthetically.

IV   The Legacy of Dada

Naturally none of this is new, although some auto-didactic artists and writers may have thought so at first. Marcel Duchamp, Kurt Schwitters and the Dadaists were exploring art through ready-mades and the *objets trouvés* or refounds, and banal imagery during the first World War. It is only recently that such artists have been given their due.

In 1959 when Robert Lebel's monograph on Marcel Duchamp appeared, it must have been a revelation. Furthermore, the Duchamp exhibition at the Guggenheim Museum surely reinforced the artists' knowledge of what had happened at the beginning of the century. It may be significant that Johns, for one, received detailed knowledge of Duchamp's work through Lebel's *catalogue raisonné*, and more than anyone he made intellectual references to Duchamp by using similar refounds or ready-mades in his work: parallels include Duchamp's *Unhappy Ready-Made* (a book) and Johns's *The Book*; a thermometer in Duchamp's *Why Not Sneeze* and Johns's *Thermometer*; and the yardstick which is common to both Duchamp's *Trois Stoppages Étalon* and Johns's *Device*.

Although Johns is an intellectually sensitive painter and Rauschenberg an intuitive and feeling one, Duchamp has meant much to both. This might be due to the growing importance now awarded to Duchamp, Schwitters and Dada after years of misunderstanding and under-estimation. Since we have all been bred on the idea that Cubism was the first and foremost revolution in twentieth-century art, it has been difficult for us to place such intellectually aesthetic artists – and the Surrealists who followed them – into our conception of contemporary art history. They have been shuffled together as side issues away from the flow of so-called 'progressive' art which has hurtled toward total abstraction. But if one takes the point of view that such 'art for art's sake' solutions are not the be-all and end-all, and that literary, psychological, poetic and reflective matter is just as valid an expression in our time, Dada and Surrealism loom large as great movements in the art of this century.

It is important to note that there are differences between what Dada professed, what it actually accomplished, and where it ended – if indeed it did end. Frequently dismissed as a nihilistic form of anti-art, it certainly aimed at a cynical refutation of accepted artistic standards of bourgeois taste and a strong criticism of contemporary movements. But as late as 1947, Georges Hugnot could write, 'Dada is ageless, it has no parent, but stands alone, making no distinction between what is and what is not. It approves while denying, it contradicts itself and acquires new force by this very contradiction . . . 'This widens the philosophical concept of Dada beyond that of the merely anarchical, destructive and anti-moral.

Hugnot, who was deeply involved with the Surrealists, based his remarks on first-hand accounts. He explained that with Dada 'there is no hope, all values are levelled to a universal monotony, there is no longer a difference between good and evil. There is only awareness. Dada is a taking stock and as such it is as irreparable as it is ridiculous. It knows only itself . . . Dada is neither modern nor modernistic, it is immediate . . . Dada utilises for its own ends what has been done already and then turns against it *threateningly*.'

And the last definition is the ultimate difference between Dada and the New Super Realism which makes the label Neo-Dada partly a misnomer. For Dada fought its battles of liberation as a sworn enemy of all existing art; it defied not only 'museum' art but the Cubists, Expressionists and Futurists. The New Super Realists refuse to fight at all, accepting everything benignly, whether popular culture, art of the present, art of the past, or the bourgeois concepts of art. There is a complacency which indicates they do not want to wipe out existing notions (whether popular or otherwise), but wish to work within the given framework. Such art does not see that the 'chance encounter of a sewing machine and an umbrella on a dissecting table', as Lautreamont suggested, is in itself beautiful: the most interesting thing would be the sewing machine, the umbrella or the dissecting table examined independently of each other. Hugnot wrote: 'Dada turns against itself, it indulges in self-destruction, it sees red, its despair is its genius.' Nobody could say that of the New Super Realism, which sits safely in its own air-cushioned armchair surveying 'coolly' and without apparent involvement the world around it.

'*Dada est mort*', said Max Ernst in 1921, '*Vive Dada!*' But in 1936 Richard Huelsenbeck was predicting 'a great future for Dada. Dada will experience a golden age, but in another form than the one imagined by the Paris Dadaists.' The Surrealists themselves, after efficiently killing off the supposedly outdated and outworn style, made use of its revolutionary new syntax in a hundred different ways. Now the New Super Realists continue to use the Dada language, although the means and ends are entirely different. It is not the style that is being revived, but the kind of freedom of attitude it initiated.

It is interesting that the point of reference between the American New Super Realists and Dada is usually made by mentioning Marcel Duchamp and Kurt Schwitters, neither of whom were purely Dada. They both worked through and beyond Tristan Tzara's Zurich movement without being much influenced or changing their ways, although they strongly influenced others. Both began their work long before the name was invented in 1916, and both continued what they were doing after its death. And, it must be remembered, it was Dada who found Duchamp, rather than the other way around.

As for Schwitters, his *Merz* works (a name derived from the word *Commerz*), which sought to combine poetry, prose, typography, advertising, plastic arts of all types and architecture, refound objects, etc., as a total and inter-related art form, could be considered a forerunner of the Environment work. *Merz* was not in the least anti-art, in fact it was very much for art, and attempted to use both traditional skills and disciplines as well as allowing the artist absolute freedom of any new techniques and materials. Both actuality and absurdity were included in this as well as facts of everyday existence. It appears now that Schwitters' *Merzbau* constructions, one of which was built inside his Hanover residence and another at Langdale, England, were extraordinarily early forerunners of the Happenings, the Environments and 'total art', all of which have had their influence on the New Super Realism. One particular collage of his, called *For Kate*, used cartoon-strip characters as cuts-outs as early as 1947.

Marcel Duchamp means much more to the Americans than Schwitters, perhaps because his *Nude Descending a Staircase* created the first 'modern art' sensation in the U.S. in 1913 at the Armory Show in New York, and brought the issue of contemporary painting to the entire American public. Also, Duchamp lived and worked in New York on and off for the rest of his life. But although he was busily hanging snow shovels and displaying bottle driers throughout the First World War, he was more intent on creating something new than destroying the old. After all, he did insist that the snow shovel and the bottle drier were actually works of art – even if only by virtue of his signature.

However, his famous urinal, called *Fontain* and sent to the new 'Independent Group' jury in New York in 1917 with the signature R. Mutt, was less a statement for the urinal as a beautiful ready-made (it is, as Rauschenberg noticed, 'very beautiful'), than a gesture to test the supposedly avant-garde jury of which he was a member and who he rightly suspected would react unfavourably toward it, because of pre-conceived notions as to what a work of art should be. Duchamp was not making an artistic case for urinals, so much as one against pre-formed notions about aesthetics. (The New Super Realists, for their part, would be neither for nor against the urinal, and hardly concerned with the jury's opinions; they would merely accept the object as a reality with artistic properties as yet unexplored). A case in point here is Duchamp's *Mona Lisa* titled *L.H.O.O.Q.* (*elle a chaud au cul*) in which her moustache does not take away from Leonardo's masterpiece as much as it adds a new dimension to the liberties one artist can take with another's work, and still produce something fresh, intelligent and amusing. Rauschenberg's *Mona Lisa* 'drawing' of 1958, done from rubbings of a print, makes no comment whatsoever on either the original work or Duchamp's version of it. He only explores what Geldzahler calls his 'own non-literal logic' to construct a sort of negative out of something overtly familiar, which in turn becomes positive again through sensitive transformation. The fact that Rauschenberg is a close friend of Duchamp may to some degree be relevant to his choosing the *Mona Lisa* for a 'drawing', but the two works are worlds apart.

Duchamp declared he was neither for art nor against it. He saw the ready-made as providing 'a form of denying the possibility for defining art' as well as a means of 'generating a new thought for the object'. But the only important thing for him, he confessed to a friend, was that 'the artist himself must be a masterpiece.' Such an awe-inspiring figure, who is currently accepted as a unique personality in art, confuses one's thoughts about his influence. Is it that we at last see the point of Duchamp because of the new art, or is it that Duchamp has made us see the new art through his example?

'Correcting' the Sapolin enamel advertisement and retitling it *Apolinère Enameled* or setting an Underwood typewriter cover on a folding stand with the description *Pliant . . . de Voyage*, may have brought Duchamp to a new means of enlarging the syntax of art, but he was not entirely alone. Francis Picabia, in New York in 1915, was producing for Stieglitz' gallery magazine *291* a series of satirical portraits; one of Max Jacob depicted him as an ordinary flashlight untransformed, and another called *Portrait d'une Jeune Fille Américaine dans l'état de Nudité*, was represented by an accurate drawing of a sparking plug. The titles of these works make their intention clear.

With such a strong background of the common object in the contemporary American art heritage, it is not surprising that the New Super Realism has rooted itself firmly on New York soil. In any event, the tradition of Realist painting has never died in New York, despite the dozens of modern art revolutions (painters like

Andrew Wyeth, John Koch, Edward Hopper and the Magic Realists still rank as important), and the combination of surviving academic traditions with the example of Duchamp was bound to produce something extraordinary when American painting swung away from total abstraction.

These facts seem just as significant as the presence of American Cubists such as Stuart Davis, Gerald Murphy and Charles Demuth, who incorporated certain poster techniques and commercial signs, symbols and labels in their works in the twenties. Like the French Cubists before them, they used such references to the commercial world either as clues for the spectator or as purely decorative elements in a total composition. Incorporated fragments of lettering or package design were part of the constructed whole; they were never substitutes for or even competitors with the artist's creations. With the New Super Realists, the basic design is usually the commercial prototype; moreover, the package or advertising symbol becomes the sum total of the work, and not just one element of it.

It is true that in paintings by Stuart Davis such as *Lucky Strike* (1921) and those by Gerald Murphy such as *Razor* (1922), the commercial imagery is so omnipresent that the over-riding impression is one of a total 'brand image'; and yet the juggling of geometry, the flat, decorative planes of synthetic Cubism carefully placed, and the playing of shapes and forms against one another give the ultimate appearance of something 'artful', which the New Super Realism is at pains to avoid.

Davis's position as the first accepted 'American' modern artist (although he worked through the French idiom) makes it evident that his old interest in billboards, common objects, advertising labels, etc., was bound to assume a new stature once art returned to commercial subject matter. Davis often admitted a sympathetic attitude to the popular culture; moreover, he confessed a lack of interest in paint quality and its application. After he executed his design there was a mechanical means of enlargement, and once he even spoke of his wish to have his pictures manufactured. He always admitted his debt to Fernand Léger, who has also been mentioned in connection with the New Super Realism, and who came to New York during the First World War and lived in a flat on New York's Bowery during the Second World War.

Léger claimed that without the 'bad taste' of New York, he would not have been able to produce the works he did. But his images were always too well manipulated and were transformed too far beyond their original models to be considered a forerunner of the new art.

With Léger, a whole pride of Surrealists settled in New York before and during the Second World War: among them Matta, Dali, Tanguy and Ernst. André Breton,

MARCEL DUCHAMP: TU M', 1918. Oil on canvas with brush attached, 27" × 122¾". Courtesy Yale University Art Gallery, bequest of Katherine S. Dreier.

the 'Pope of Surrealism', who began as a Dada-ist, also came to New York, and with Ernst and Duchamp founded a magazine called *VVV*. Once more the language of Dada, transformed through Surrealism into something positive and powerful, came alive, and it now seems that artists such as Dine, Oldenburg, Wesselmann and Rosenquist would be very different if it had not been for the Surrealists. Particularly in Oldenburg, an element of bizarre unreality is introduced by his enlargement of hamburgers or french fries to Alice in Wonderland proportions, which might not have been possible if the Surrealists had not pointed the way.

There is, however, one particular aspect of New York's New Super Realism that is wholly American: the food aspect. In a review of an Environment exhibition called the *Supermarket Show* in 1964, *Life* magazine commented: 'Supermarket food is so American. The great production belt of our largest industry overwhelms us at every season of the year with gorgeously coloured, bigger than life-size comestibles, and if the frozen-in flavor of wax beans sometimes turns out to be the flavor of wax, this is all part of the world's highest standard of living.'

Perhaps it is for this reason that American Pop-ists have concentrated deeply on supermarket or drug-store food. Wayne Thiebaud paints 'popsicles' (a kind of over-sweetened ice on a stick), and rows of layer cake and sandwiches in glass cases; Andy Warhol paints soup tins; Jasper Johns casts beer cans; Robert Indiana constructs electric-light 'EAT' signs; Roy Lichtenstein does comic strip versions of ice-cream sodas; Tom Wesselmann constructs huge plastic oranges, soda-pop bottles and stacks of display food. And Oldenburg models window display 'Sundaes' (dishes of ice cream with mixed flavours, covered with whipped cream and cherries) in plaster of Paris, as well as hamburgers with pickles and tomatoes, and even arranges a real gas stove with plaster reproductions of pots of food, roasts and vegetables.

The obsession in American New Super Realism with food cannot be ignored. It has been analysed by the Freudians who claim it has something to do with bottle feeding instead of breast feeding by American mothers (a majority of the objects are ones that are sucked or nibbled at); it has been explained by sociologists who give statistics as to how much leisure time and interest is spent on food in the U.S.; and it is pondered over by economists who see food production as the one stable factor in American spending.

But art critics are eager to dismiss the significance of such subject matter. D. G. Seckler writing on 'The Folklore of the Banal'* in *Art in America* pointed out that when we look at a still life 'we do not ask whether Cézanne enjoyed eating apples'. It would seem however, that the pre-packaged food of America, the tins,

* Here the term is used in its original etymological sense, meaning 'common to all'.

YVES KLEIN: UNTITLED, 1957. *Sponge, 47½" high, base 7¼".*
Courtesy Mr Robert Fraser.

The New Super Realism has not been limited to New York and London, although that is where it has made its greatest impact. The *Nouveau Réalisme* of Paris has some links with the new art, but they appear superficial on the whole. Yves Klein's monochromes and Hains's and Villeglé's 'lacerated posters' which date back to 1949, are in some sense related. Arman's accumulations and dissections of common objects, Martial Raysse's compartmentalised 'boxes' and assemblages (one of which includes a live bathing beauty) reflect the new art.

Among the most inventive of the French group is Alain Jacquet; his *camouflages* reproduce paintings such as Michelangelo's *Pieta* or Bronzino's *Cupid and Venus*. Disguised with bright shreds of colour, such subjects create a puzzling disparity between the remembered original and the abstraction superimposed. Jacquet has re-done Manet's *Déjeuner sur l'Herbe* (itself a re-do of Marcantonio's print of Raphael's *Judgement of Paris*) by photographing a group by a swimming pool, and then blowing it up until the grain-dots obscure the image; it is then silk-screened in large editions, and further cut up with details enlarged again until there is little left of the original figuration. Jacquet feels he ought to produce only one painting a year, with all its various enlargements and developments, and says ideally the pictures ought to be sold at department stores such as Macy's.

Another young group in Paris is the *Poulet 2ONF*, composed of three artists, Smerck, Sanejouand and Chabaud. Smerck and Chabaud use news photography close-ups and repeats, while Sanejouand juxtaposes made-up and ready-made objects with startling originality, in the tradition of Surrealism.

The Italians Rotella and Mario Schifano have taken the billboard with its torn accumulation of posters as a source of inspiration; Tano Festa does versions of photo-print reproductions of old masters, reminiscent perhaps of cheap Medici prints; Moretti in Florence has used pornography without compunction, and a naked woman stamped over with the word 'Végé' (the sign of the Common Market) leaves little to the imagination, as do his tawdry billboards and bedroom suites. Oyvind Fahlstrom from Sweden uses cartoon cut-outs to make overall abstractions, and has used such designs as Batman's Cloak, from the comics.

Many of these artists have employed the commonplace as an expedient to a type of abstraction, where the commercial image is only reproduced to make a dramatic, decorative effect rather than to create an ambiguity or to be examined obsessively. But ready-made imagery and objects are perhaps not entirely at home in European art (as we have seen with the British), particularly not in Paris, where the conscious awareness of 'art history' makes the use of the banal almost meretricious.

Pierre Restany, who has been involved in writing manifestoes and codifying the theories of *Nouveau Réalisme* since 1960, seems determined to link the Paris artists to the New Super Realists. He sees a strong connection between Klein, Tinguely, Arman and César, not only with Rauschenberg, Johns, Lichtenstein and Oldenburg, but with such Americans as Chamberlain, Conner and Stankiewicz. He does not make the necessary distinction between the constructionists, the assemblers, and the aleatory artists who depend entirely on chance effects. All might employ the ad-mass commonplace, but is is only when used specifically and pinned directly to some exploration of the object, as itself, that it qualifies for the New Super Realism: it is not a question of just turning teacups and telephones into 'beautiful' abstractions; the objects must keep their ugly identity while still being transformed into something new.

By including artists such as Lichtenstein and Oldenburg in his compendium of 'Neo-Dada', M. Restany creates a confusion of purpose and point of view. Curiously, he still feels that the Americans are involved with protest, provocation and rejection, and he thinks they work through an 'observance of a traditional aestheticism'. This denies the empirical nature of their art, and one gets the idea that he is expressing what he feels Americans ought to be doing, rather than what they are actually involved with. But if, as he says, *Nouveau Réalisme* is a sort of 'Industrial neo-Baroque', then Johns, Rauschenberg, Oldenburg and Lichtenstein have little to do with it, for they are not concerned with creating a unified style as much as they are with stating new emotional and ideational factors about commonplace reality.

The New Super Realists have, through their experiments, continuously asked, 'What is art?' Moreover, they have asked it in terms of a whole new cultural *milieu* which they have come to accept as an undeniable fact. Such enquiries have, of necessity, meant the re-introduction of subject matter, which itself is a precarious, nerve-wracking affair after half a century of abstraction. For, having attempted to teach ourselves not to see the figurative in abstractions, can our eyes now only

ALAIN JACQUET: MAN'S PORTRAIT (FROM DEJEUNER SUR L'HERBE), 1964. *Silk screen*, $8\frac{1}{8}'' \times 6\frac{1}{4}''$. *Courtesy of the artist, Paris.*

MIMMO ROTELLA: MARILYN DECOLLAGE, 1963. *50" × 38" (app). Courtesy Galerie 'J', Paris.*

ALBERTO MORETTI: VEGE, 1964. *Oil on canvas, collage, 58" × 44". Courtesy of the artist, Florence.*

OYVIND FAHLSTROM: THE COLD WAR (VARIABLE POINTS, 1964), PHASE I, 1964 (detail). *Tempera on plastic and metal on 2 metal panels. Complete work 5′ × 8′ + 5′ × 8′. Collection Mr Oliver Baker, New York.*

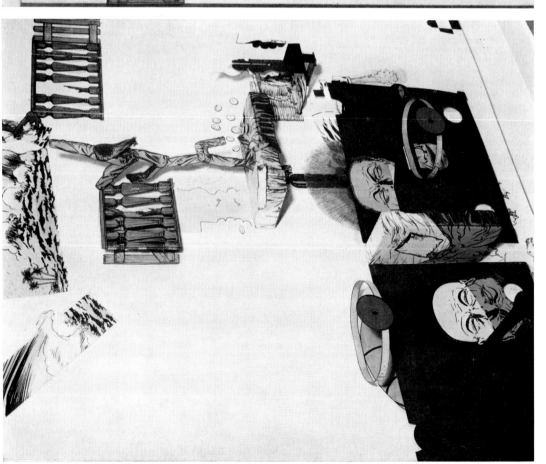

OYVIND FAHLSTROM: THE COLD WAR, PHASE 3, (detail), 1964. *Tempera on plastic and metal on 2 metal panels. Complete work, 5′ × 8′ + 5′ × 8′. Collection Mr Oliver Baker, New York.*

see abstractions when we look at the figurative? Such a complex situation in contemporary art must be taken into account.

As a generation fed on 'difficult' art, we can easily feel we are being cheated of a real art experience if the new art looks too 'easy' because of its recognizable forms and its commonly understood symbols and styles. Perhaps for this reason the New Super Realists deplore total emphasis on the subjects of their choice, and deny all psychological or sociological interpretations in their works. They insist that we are to look at them for and by themselves, without any ready reference at hand to explain them away; their contention is that if they 'mean' something socially significant, that is our business, not theirs.

Such intentions are supported by several critics, who feel we can wrongly be led to creating 'stories' to accompany images, and thus be guilty of over-interpreting paintings because their contemporary images might imply something 'significant' or start a train of literal thought. Swenson, for one, feels that, having acquired what he calls 'the habits of abstraction', we have begun to see it in all the paintings we know, even if they are patently figurative. It is not so much a question of choosing to do so, since for those of us who have been brought up in the 'fifties with Abstract Expressionism it is impossible to do otherwise.

Similar arguments have been advanced for the restoration to favour of some nineteenth-century art, particularly that of the Pre-Raphaelites and the *Salon* painters. The subject matter in a Burne-Jones, an Alma Tadema, a Bouguereau, now considered without meaning (except nostalgically), is therefore reduced to a mere excuse for enjoying a piece of painting of exquisite refinement and sophistication on a purely formal, or abstract level.

It is true that a tension between abstraction and representation in any work of art has often been the one quality that makes it live through changes in fashionable iconography. Just as one can now find abstract design in a Carracci or a Luca Giordano, where the descriptive content may no longer be significant or immediate, so we can often imagine, or conjure up, figurative messages in a Jackson Pollock or a Sam Francis. But the subtlety of this argument would appear to belie the clear and simple facts. When the figurative elements are so strongly bound to the contemporary scene, and are so definitely linked to commonly understood things which we all experience daily, it would be a fallacy to suppose that we could eradicate or even reduce the power of such literary content for the advantage of seeing the formal aspects alone. The best works will surely be the ones where the representational and the formal qualities so complement each other that neither can be read or experienced independently, but both are bound together inseparably.

VI   And After?

Where is the new art going? What is its future? For five years critics have said
with conviction that it is on its way out, and for five years it has returned each
season, more deeply entrenched in our consciousness. For, whatever we think
about it, the fact is that we do have to think about it. Although it may lose its
fashionable place – and what movement does not? – its point and purpose cannot
be denied. Like all useful art, it has changed our visions and attitudes about the
world we live in, and we will never see things in the same way again. Which of
us can look at a soup tin, a package of cigarettes, a subway advertisement without
new intensity, in a new light or without a new frame of reference? As an art that
sets out to reflect its own time, it has sliced into our culture with razor sharpness
and left the segments for us to examine.

And not only the critics and collectors are taking the New Super Realism to heart.
By mid-1965, Pop Art has invaded life in a number of ways as no other art style
has done with the exception of Op Art: not only Pop refrigerators with comic
cartoons painted on them, but giant zippers and huge ties which drape over ladies'
dresses, have appeared as well as Campbell soup tins on evening gowns. A full page
advertisement in the *New York Times* offers Pop Art pictures of favourite comic
strip heroes such as the Phantom or Superman for $ 3.98 ('They're underselling me'
says Roy Lichtenstein, 'but it's just great!'). Supermarket attendants are plagued
for 'real' Brillo boxes by suburban housewives; display companies sell heretofore
useless, out of date, advertising signs for large sums (especially those with optic
double-image effects); old comic books have become collectors' items, with some
rare numbers selling for as much as $ 100.

The *New York Herald Tribune* in a bid for stylishness produced a Sunday supplement
which exclaimed through the convention of a cartoon balloon: '*Pop go the clothes*
What starts with *Pop* Art, like Andy Warhol's tomato soup cans has suddenly
become *Pop* living! It's the far out in fashion, decorating, design and beauty

crocheted sweatshirts, jack of hearts refrigerators, the 13 most beautiful girls in underground movies, the High Camp look of lucite furniture. It's what this issue is all about!'

Such a fantastic absorption by the ad-mass world of an art form originally intended for a sophisticated few must indicate a certain will on the part of the public to accept the use of the banal and the commercial in pseudo-art and its quick-change fashion by-products. In over five years, an *avant garde* movement has fed the makers of *avant kitsch* but still continues to be vital means of artistic expression.

Dame Edith Sitwell, in a letter of protest to *The Times Literary Supplement* against William Burrough's *The Naked Lunch*, said, 'I do not want to spend the rest of my life with my nose nailed to other people's lavatories.' But that is in a sense what Pop is about. Our noses are visually being nailed to what we have been taught to regard as hideous, loathsome, vulgar, and cheap in the popular culture. This is not done out of perversity or amorality but because there is a strong desire to establish a dialogue between the ever-present ad-mass world and the debilitated world of fine art. Such a dialogue is perhaps a necessity if the arts themselves are to survive as a viable and significant element in society.

It will be years before we can determine the true significance of such an art, and at the moment it would be reckless to come to pat conclusions about its longevity. Even more than other movements, it is, by its nature, transitory and ephemeral, and already many of its artists have either intensified their ideas or moved on to something which is more personal to them. But as a point of departure, it is an exciting, vigorous new art, packed with image-ideas which can be expanded, exploded and dropped at will when they have lost their impact and immediacy. The ever-present, ever-growing ad-mass culture will see to it that there are others to take their place.

Most of all, it has dutifully worked within the precepts of a time which demands that its art be either amazing or amusing. The New Super Realism manages to be both.

D. SMERCK: J'AIME TROP GEMEY, 1964. *Oil on canvas, 76" × 58". Collection M. and Mme J. Y. Noury, Paris.*

RAYMOND HAINS: CET HOMME EST DANGEREUX, 1965. *Collage, Courtesy Galerie 'J', Paris.*

Principal Artists

United States

JIM DINE

ROBERT INDIANA

ROY LICHTENSTEIN

CLAES OLDENBURG

JAMES ROSENQUIST

GEORGE SEGAL

ANDY WARHOL

TOM WESSELMANN

Great Britain

PETER BLAKE

PATRICK CAULFIELD

DAVID HOCKNEY

ALLEN JONES

GERALD LAING

PETER PHILLIPS

Anglo-American

RICHARD SMITH

R. B. KITAJ

Since Richard Smith lives and works in New York much of the time, and since he was first exhibited by a New York gallery, he does not cleanly fit into the British or American movement, although he was involved with Pop Art's beginnings in London. By the same token, since American R. B. Kitaj studied painting in England, had his first showing there and lives permanently in London, he cannot be placed in the American movement, although his work is extremely American in feeling, just as Smith's sensibility could only be English.

77

United States

JIM DINE

Jim Dine's pictures combine both the vocabulary of paint and the vocubalary of images in such a way that they confront each other in his works on equal terms and as complements. For instance, if he attaches a shower nozzle to a flat canvas, the expressionist brush strokes will take on the appearance of a spray of water, just as much as the nozzle will seem to be an extension of the formal qualities of the paint. The word 'shower' painted into the canvas, will add a further definition. Equally, a lawn-mower attached to his canvas will be 'connected' to the paint surface by green strokes which might remind us of grass. As literal as these images sound, they actually create a confusion of facts. Are we looking at an object or a subject?

There appears to be a connection here between the painterly hang-over of Abstract Expressionism and the re-discovered Ready-Made; but unlike that of Rauschenberg or Johns, there is no poetic free association in Dine's imagery: he must define explicitly what he is doing in terms of the paint, the attached object and its word symbol. He believes it is better for him to start with a concrete, recognizable object, using the object or idea as catalyst until it becomes something else.

It has been said that these works seek to break the space between the spectator and the art creation (much the way a Happening does), but it is clear that Dine is perversely attached to the easel picture, and every object fixed to his canvases, whether a dressing gown, a lawn-mower or a washbasin, confirms his absolute need for the picture plane, to which his objects are unalterably connected and without which they would mean nothing.

Why Dine feels the need to employ such rigid ready-mades as a light-bulb, a chest of drawers or a medicine cabinet might be explained by his feeling that 'the canvas is the last vestige of unreality ... It is so unrealistic to put that washbasin on canvas that I have to do it.'

Close to Abstract Expressionism in the handling of his paint and his use of 'gestural' marks, Dine says, 'I don't believe there was a sharp break and this is replacing Abstract

Expressionism ... Pop art is only one facet of my work. More than popular images, I'm interested in personal images, in making paintings about my studio, my experience as a painter, about painting itself.'

Although he does not feel he is related directly to Dada, he says, 'I never saw any reason to laugh at that stuff. It seemed the most natural thing in the world to have a fur-lined teacup. I thought it was just a beautiful object; it wasn't anti-art at all.'

He says that Abstract Expressionism was a strong influence on his work, particularly Motherwell's painting: 'I think he's continually growing and making problems. His paintings mean a lot to me ...'

For him, problems in art are more important than the solutions: 'I paint about problems of how to make a picture work, the problems of seeing, of making people aware without handing it to them on a silver platter.' Moreover, he believes: 'the statement about bridging the gap between art and life is, I think, a very nice metaphor or image, if that's what you'd call it, but I don't believe it ... If the object is used, then people say the object is used to bridge the gap – it's crazy. The object is used to make art, just like paint is used to make art.'

Asked whether the New Super Realism makes a 'comment' or not, Dine says, 'If it's art, who cares if it's a comment? I'm involved with formal elements. You've got to be; I can't help it. But any work of art, if it's successful, is going to be a comment on what it's about.'

Dine, like Wesselmann, comes from Cincinnati. He was born in 1935, and is a graduate of the University of Cincinnati and the Boston Museum School. He shared his first New York show in 1958 at the Judson Gallery with Wesselmann, and in 1960 did an Environment exhibition called *The House* together with Oldenburg's *The Street*. In 1962, his exhibition at Martha Jackson's gallery brought him to prominence. The same year he appeared in Sidney Janis' *New Realists* show.

It is interesting that he has been the last of the American group to receive acceptance, probably because, while his objects are harsh and unmalleable, the canvases to which they are attached are so entirely painterly that critical judgement is once more puzzled by the ambiguity of a multiple statement.

ROBERT INDIANA

One of the few New Super Realists who believe emphatically that the new art heralds a dramatic break with the past, Robert Indiana is perhaps the 'coolest' – at first glance. But his huge 'signs' resembling highway directions, which order one to EAT, ERR or DIE, although they have a slick surface attraction, possess something deep and troubling beneath their road-sign simplicity.

The words themselves transmit a psychological and emotional jolt and the artist appears to want them to gnaw into the subconscious and to come to terms with associations, past and present. For instance, his YIELD BROTHER, stencilled carefully on to canvas, is not only planned to work in the context of the design but is intended to conjure up any number of personal remembrances: i.e., brotherly love, the Bible, big brother. Words such as EAT and DIE are self-explanatory.

Working in a Hard Edge style which might facetiously be called Poptical, Indiana associates colours which are bound to jar against each other: Day-Glo red against Kelly green, against searing blue. The effects are extraordinary, and the word DIE reverberates with an uncanny aliveness while the word EAT funnels away from us as if we have sped past it on an expressway.

Indiana, whose name is a pseudonym taken from the state where he was born, believes that Pop constitutes a sort of 'new ash-can school' - deliberately striving to wipe out art for art's sake. 'The word plasticity,' he says, 'gives me a chill,' and he carefully works and reworks a painting to create a flat, hard-edged image and even tone of colour, which has no trace of the artist's fine brushwork.

Anonymity is one of his goals, as he sees it all around him. The growing impersonality and sameness of a glass city do not bother him, and he claims that, if given the chance, 'I would love to have a studio on the top of the Empire State Building.'

'I don't want to be a machine like Warhol,' he says, 'but I would not hesitate using a machine. I still use a brush because I have not found a machine inexpensive enough to take its place. I love the idea of a machine working for me; the trouble is, where

ROBERT INDIANA: THE BLACK YIELD BROTHER 3, 1963. *Oil on canvas, 85" × 85". Collection Mr. John G. Powers, New Jersey. (To be viewed diagonally.)*

ROBERT INDIANA: EAT-DIE, 1962. *Oil on canvas, diptych; each panel 72" × 60". Courtesy Stable Gallery, New York.*

JIM DINE: LARGE SHOWER NUMBER 1, 1962. *Oil on canvas, metal and rubber, 72″ × 48″. Collection Mr and Mrs Robert Mayer, Illinois.*

ROY LICHTENSTEIN: DROWNING GIRL, 1963. *Oil, magna, canvas, 68″ × 68″. Collection Mr and Mrs C. B. Wright, Seattle, Washington.*

does one draw the line? You could wake up one morning and find you are working for the machine.'

Born in New Castle, Indiana, in 1928, as Robert Clarke he studied at John Herron Art Institute in Indianapolis just after the war, then moved on to the Munson-Williams Proctor Institute, Utica, New York, to the Chicago Art Institute, and finally to the Edinburgh College of Art, 1953 - 54.

When he first arrived on Manhattan's lower East Side in 1956, 'with no particular interest in the mid-town wave of Abstract Expressionism', he took a loft on Coenties Slip in a nineteenth century building which used to be a ship's Chandler's shop. A brass stencil discovered in a corner of the loft gave him the chance to use it as a legend on a canvas, and he started painting other legends from discovered stencils. He now stencils literary references from Whitman and Hart Crane, as well as names of long-forgotten companies and, of course, his three-letter directives.

His style perhaps relates most closely to the hard-edge works of Charles Sheeler, Stuart Davis, Demuth and other U.S. precisionists, but more specifically to those of Ellsworth Kelly who once had a studio nearby. Kelly, as an outsider at the time of the Abstract Expressionist reign, joined with a group of friends, including Jack Younger-man and James Rosenquist (all living at Coenties Slip at that time, with Rauschenberg and Johns nearby), who were not in sympathy with the emotionally expressive 'gestural' painting of the 'fifties.

Indiana's geometric forms, circles, squares, rectangles, diamonds have moved a long way from some of the earlier works which were clearly related to the stark Hard Edge school of Kelly and Youngerman. He admits that afternoons spent drawing with Kelly impressed him and he was much taken by Kelly's clean, precise style. Even his series of figure paintings of Mother and Father posed by a Model-T Ford have the schematic, hard-edge appearance of this style which was so influential.

Indiana believes that Pop is an easy art form: 'Pop is Instant art . . . its comprehension can be as immediate as a crucifixion. Its appeal may be as broad as its range; it is the wide screen of the Late Show. It is not the Latin of the hierarchy, it is the vulgar.'

He believes the American Myth is, to a large degree, at the bottom of all New Super Realism – whether in London, Paris, or Hong Kong, but admits there is an element of cynicism in the use of such a myth. Speaking for himself, he says: 'It is pretty hard to swallow the whole thing about the American Dream' (which he has stencilled across several canvases). 'It started from the day the Pilgrims landed, the dream, the idea that Americans have more to eat than anyone else. But I remember going to bed without enough to eat.'

As for the importance of popular culture in our time, he believes that 'When the

ROY LICHTENSTEIN: PISTOL, 1964. *Banner in tempera, felt, made by the Betsy Ross American Flag and Banner Co, 82" × 49". Courtesy Leo Castelli Gallery, New York.*

remains of our civilisation are dug up in a thousand years, it will be our washing machines more than the contents of our museums which will define our culture.'

Roy Lichtenstein employs the classical method of 'quoting' commonly accepted prototypes, in much the same way as the Romans copied the Greeks or the Renaissance copied the Romans; the difference is that he uses the language of today. Moreover, he allows his expressions of sentiment or emotion to be harnessed to a restricted technique which is totally unemotional, in the same way that 'Ideal' models might have been handled by Ingres or David. But his ideal types are contemporary, popular ones, taken from the 'Classics' comic-book idiom.

While Warhol produces a sensation or feeling from his news-photo images, Lichtenstein aims at wrenching, from the most unlikely sources, an astonishing array of formal designs. Using imagery which has already been rendered two-dimensional by a previous commercial hand, he works within a self-limitation that would appear to leave no room for manipulation; yet he manages within that chosen restriction to produce works of great strength and subtlety.

Comparisons which have been made between Lichtenstein and Courbet are somewhat misconceived, since Courbet's use of the popular *Images d'Epinal* was totally conceptual (the *Burial at Ornans* had to do with a provincial funeral, not the popular image of one), and was based on an idea of bringing fine art to the masses on an understandable 'realistic' level. A closer parallel may be the dissatisfaction experienced by both artists with the accepted styles of their time, in favour of low subject matter and vulgar style.

Also, Lichtenstein is not interested in 'realism' as such; he appears to be more determined to make abstractions out of the figurative, without losing the content of the subject matter. In his most successful works, the blown-up scale and enlarged mechanical dots become so formal that the subject matter is almost obscured: a tension is set up between the recognizable image and the formal design almost to the point where both become one, thus solving the argument of figurative versus abstract on his own terms.

Born in New York in 1923, Lichtenstein grew up at the time when the comic book was a cultural phenomenon in the U.S.: sex, sentimentality and sadism, as expressed in the adventures of Captain Marvel; Superman; Wonderwoman; Flash Gordon; Sheena, Queen of the Jungle; Tarzan; Batman and Robin; and others (all popular manifestations of late Surrealism). Some time later, the war comic book emerged, with its tales of terror and torture, as well as the romance comic book, with sentimental stories of passion, infidelity, unrequited love and betrayal – much in the manner of Victorian *genre* painting.

After gaining brief experience in industrial design and display work in Ohio, Lichtenstein earned his master's degree in fine arts at Ohio State University. Earlier, he had done some experimenting with comic book designs as the basis for Abstract Expressionist painting, and his first comic-book subjects included Popeye, Mickey Mouse, and cowboys and indians.

Lichtenstein's works have caused confusion and concern since they are so close to their originals – medium and scale apart – that one must look two or three times to be certain they are not direct enlargements of a strip-cartoon image.

According to the mannerism and eccentricities of the original, the artist exaggerates and refines what he discovers until the stereotyped emotional expressions of sentiments are stripped bare and brutally exposed, allowing the formal elements to rise to the surface. The flat comic-strip style, which denies spatial depth, yet quotes the conventions of cartoon space, the ungainly black lines that encircle the forms, the vulgar primary colours, may at first disguise the potential beauty hidden in such raw material. But everything is exploited by the artist: the Art Nouveau curves of a woman's tresses, the angled elegance of a man's hand holding a pistol, the mysterious forms lurking in an exploded fighter-plane, or the stylised waves over a drowning girl – which remind one of the formal conventions of Japanese art.

The Ben Day dot technique, a screen of minute dots which make up the colour shading in a comic strip, is in itself an inventive means of pattern-making, and when enlarged becomes so decorative that it has lured misguided critics into comparisons with *pointillisme* and Signac. Such dots have a mechanical accuracy and a cold regularity that belie the emotional or sentimental content of the imagery. Thus, the artist not only uses the mechanical art process for formal ends but makes a virtue of the *clichés* of the original drawing. What is more, with such rich subject matter he can at the same time indirectly imply an ironic comment or indulge in satire.

Although his art has been defended as subtle 'transformation', Lichtenstein says, 'I think my work is different from comic strips – but I wouldn't call it transformation. . . The comics have shapes but there has been no effort to make them intensely unified.

JAMES ROSENQUIST: VESTIGIAL APPENDAGE, 1962. *Oil on canvas, 72" × 93". Courtesy Green Gallery.*

89

CLAES OLDENBURG: 7 up, 1961. *Painted plaster wall projection, 56" × 36". Collection Mr and Mrs Burton Tremaine, New York.*

The purpose is different; one intends to depict and I intend to unify'.

It is amusing to note that the professional comic artists are eager to disclaim Lichtenstein as a copyist, and a National Periodical Publications meeting in the U.S. judged his works as definitely not mirror images of current comic styles. The professionals regarded his works as 'strongly "decorative" and backward looking.'

Lichtenstein likes the contradiction between the violence, emotion and passion in his subjects, and the mechanical and removed style they are expressed in: 'To express this thing in a painterly style would dilute it; the techniques I use are not commercial, they only appear to be commercial.'

He insists ,'The meaning of my work is that it's industrial, it's what all the world will soon become. Europe will be the same way, soon, so it won't be American; it will just be universal.'

Lichtenstein's landscapes of 1964 bear out this point of view: the paintings are composed of industrial products such as glass, or multi-lens Rowlux plastic sheeting, made up of dots or of a *voile* sheen with an undulating texture, which moves as the spectator moves. He has 'printed' other landscapes and comic strip images, on huge porcelain enamel sheets, in small editions, and he has designed an edition of felt 'banners' made up by the Betsy Ross American Flag and Banner Company.

But the strange thing about Lichtenstein's work is that, industrial though he wants it to be, only he seems able to re-produce it in proper scale and material. When seen in a magazine reproduction it is merely returned to its original source.

Oldenburg has attempted to equate 'ideas' with physical forms, much the way Andy Warhol tries to equate 'feelings' with images. His objects in three-dimension, whether food, or mass-produced items, have strong literary associations which the artist carries out in the most painterly way. His works are more like sculpted paintings than painted sculptures, since it is the paint surface, the colour and the design that make the forms viable. He is concerned not with spatial considerations or with sculptural manipulation, as in traditional sculpture, but only with what has been called the 'object-quality' of the piece itself.

His objects are handled expressionistically, and any given area of an Oldenburg Hamburger or Ice Cream Sundae, taken out of context, might be thought to be an Abstract Expressionist picture surface, so rich and alive is the paint quality, so freely applied and active is the colour. The fact that the surfaces themselves are roughly worked, also ties him to the Action Painting of the 'fifties.

It has been said that his food 'sculptures', particularly the Ice Cream Sundaes, Hamburgers, Chocolate Eclairs, Pecan Pies, Hot Dogs, and so forth, are 'filled with the joy of sensation, mouthwatering, and brightly enamelled.' But that is to over-simplify their power: the sheer vulgarity and tastelessness of such objects, in direct contradiction to nostalgic associations with childhood or fun-fair eating, makes them repulsive to the eye while they bring to the subconscious salivary memories of the past.

Two nightmare reactions might in fact take place when looking at an Oldenburg food-object: the sated could feel nausea, while the under-privileged could once more feel like the child pressing his nose at the window of the ice-cream parlour.

Oldenburg is only interested in the commonplace or the advertising image indirectly (he has, however, done a 7 Up sign and a Coca-Cola label); rather, his objects refer to the pre-cooked drugstore variety, as cut-rate as any other item in the shop. Such food reminds one not so much of the edible as of reproductions of the edible. For instance, the Ice Cream Sundae, with dripping whipped cream and a cherry on top, recalls the fake display in a sweet-shop window, rather than the original served on the counter. There is something consciously synthetic about the shiny enamel colours and the free drips of paint, which makes these objects totally unappetising.

Born in Stockholm in 1929, Oldenburg was brought up in Chicago, as the son of the Swedish Consul-General. A graduate of Yale, he took a degree in English, and became a newspaper reporter in Chicago. He started art late in life, and after studying at the Chicago Institute of Art moved to New York in 1956. His first New York show was at the Judson Gallery, and in 1960 he presented his first Environment exhibition, *The Street*, together with Jim Dine's *The House*. Called the *Ray Gun Show*, it concluded with a number of Happenings. In 1961, the Martha Jackson Gallery presented his first version of *The Store*, an exhibition made up of make-believe food.

'*The Street* is cold, *The Store* is warm,' he says, 'while *The Street* is reality and *The Store* is unreality.' He considers *The Store* 'a dream' as well as the food in it: 'Nobody could ever make a cake look the way it looks in an ice-box.' This ambiguity of almost-real and not-real is what he is striving for: 'Some came in (to *The Store*) and said, "This is not art, it's a hamburger"; and others said, "This is not a hamburger, it's art."' Thus, he feels he succeeded in producing something 'halfway between art and life,' since 'nothing is interesting to me unless it is halfway . . .'

In more recent works, Oldenburg has made his objects in Vinyl plastic and in canvas, perhaps to reduce the personal expressionist quality. His French Fries are blown up to Brobdingnagian proportions; sewn together by his wife, the gigantic potato straws filled with Kapok are movable and soft to the touch – like huge cushions. They are arranged any way one likes, with a large dollop of red ketchup on top, also in cuddly, Kapok-stuffed washable Vinyl.

His soft typewriters in the same material, and his soft toasters in canvas (which look deflated and formless) and his blown up tube of toothpaste in wood, lacquer, metal, rubber, Vinyl, Kapok and cloth, connect him more directly with a kind of advanced Surrealism, where the ordinary object is made fantastic both by exaggeration and by a sudden juxtaposition with the real world.

Oldenburg admits he has a 'fascination with the limitation of what is beautiful and what people have to work with in a mass-produced society.'

In another age, Rosenquist might have been a leading Academician. Using a technique he learned as a billboard painter, he has a method as slick as any 19th century *Salon* artist whose style has unwittingly been preserved in today's commercial sign painting. Both imperceptible modelling of form from light to dark and an almost standardised rendition of anatomy (based not on observation of reality but on observation of previous art styles) characterise his work.

But Rosenquist's palette is strictly that of the commercial billboard, with its rancid sweet blues, pale pinks, bland greens and greys. Such sickly-saccharine colouring fills in knife-sharp contours and steel-like definitions in his huge canvases, which cut the picture plane into hard segments that are unrelated to each other, except formally.

And it is in such fragmentation that Rosenquist achieves something remarkable. For, in disregarding depth, and handling his perspective arbitrarily, he creates a kind of ambiguity between the highly 'realistic', almost academic, forms, and the effect of total abstraction he achieves with them. A leg, a pair of spectacles, a car fender or a piece of cake, when enlarged to giant proportions and irrationally sliced into fragments, takes on an entirely new condition, relative to the painting in which it is incorporated rather than to its former position in the real world.

Of all the New Super Realists, Rosenquist is most keen to disregard cause and effect, logic and a sense of sequence. There is no beginning, middle and end in his works; they just start and stop. These huge walls of canvas are in a way related to the Abstract Expressionist's 'totality' of the field of vision, which is continuous and all-encompassing. To be in a gallery filled entirely with his work is indeed a strange sensation, perhaps close to the feeling Rosenquist himself experienced when he was a professional billboard painter.

Born in North Dakota in 1933, he studied at the Arts Students League in New York while working for the General Outdoor Advertising Company. It was while painting the enormous billboards thirty stories above Times Square that he suddenly saw the commonplace things he was doing in a new perspective. The subjects themselves were so large that they took on a new character, and a face twenty-five feet wide by thirty-five feet high became a cloud of graduating pinks, half recognizable and yet distinctly abstracted from reality.

Working on the thirty-by-one-hundred foot Astor-Victoria billboard at Times Square, he says, 'gave me the opportunity to see things in a new relationship.' The delineation of some part of painted anatomy, or some giant piece of lettering, would appear to him as a 'line trailing. You couldn't see the whole thing at once; it was like infinity.' When he was painting an enormous area of bright red, the colour saturation was so intense that when he looked down from his scaffolding to the traffic below, 'Everything looked different.'

Rosenquist's work, reminiscent of a wide-angle movie screen, seems close to Surrealism with its Freudian free association of common and hateful images. The artist clearly does not like what he paints, but he sticks to his subject/objects with a dogged determination until he finds something in them of value. Alan Solomon feels that the artist, 'has not only made the cosmetic bearable, but has found the detachment to see it aesthetically, that is, to perceive that even something fraudulent – in spirit and body – can have a pictorial beauty.'

His chosen images are not what the artist calls 'hot-blooded images' but things just far enough removed from the present to be seen dispassionately. In 1960, for instance, he would have painted a 1950 Ford fender: 'I paint anonymous things in the hopes that their particular meanings will disappear... I use images from old magazines – when I say old, I mean 1945 to 1955 – a time we haven't started to ferret out as history yet.' He feels such images are 'no images', without any nostalgic or immediate presence: 'There is a freedom there. If it were abstract, people might make it into something. If you paint Franco-American spaghetti, they won't make a crucifixion out of it, and also who could be nostalgic about canned spaghetti?'

He admits, 'I treat the billboard image as it is, so apart from nature. I paint it as a reproduction of other things; I try to get as far away from nature as possible.' One of Rosenquist's earliest works is called *Flower Garden*, a large canvas containing an athlete's torso, supported by an arm, with three hands equal in scale to the figure, thrust up from the bottom edge of the painting into the anonymous grey space that unites them all. Such a work, taken with its title, looks specifically Surrealist. He has made a 'painting' out of coloured bits of string criss-crossing through an open space, and has put together a 'canvas' of a tree by threading the canvas into the real tree, as if the tree had outgrown the canvas (this recalls Magritte). However, his three-dimensional works are not entirely successful; his virtuoso handling of two-dimensional illusion and his brilliant ability to compose with structural conviction are best expressed on the flat, rectangular picture plane.

As for his subjects in his pictures, he insists, 'The subject matter isn't popular images; it isn't that at all.'

GEORGE SEGAL

The works of George Segal defy traditional definition. Are they sculptures, Environments, assemblages, casts, or all four combined? Segal's plaster figures, done from live human beings, are reminiscent of the lava-preserved corpses left at Pompei; arrested in the most ordinary occupations, they are like living forms caught at a moment in time, as they might be when a movie-camera suddenly stops. Always in their own Environment setting, with its tawdry fittings and furnishings, they demand that we measure them as they exist in the scale and space of the real world; yet they declare themselves works of art. A bus driver at his wheel, a woman in a cafeteria booth, a couple intertwined in intercourse, someone riding a bicycle, and even a workman changing the lettering on a cinema marquee are subjects that Segal has dealt with. These lonely, forlorn people, rough-cast in wet plaster, are not finished to look real; that is, there is no attempt at natural colouring or illusionistic surface, since they are always white. But their surroundings, such as a token machine, an iron bedstead, table and chairs, a pinball machine, are from the real world. Here again is the *leit-motif* of the New Super Realism: a personal questioning of the nature of reality and art.

The nostalgic quality and literary overtones in Segal's works make him appear to be a direct descendant of nineteenth century *genre* painting and, as in *genre* painting, there is no small element of sentiment in his subject matter. The pathos or loneliness of the figures, against their commonplace 'props' and surroundings, is objectified like a picture by Edward Hopper, but it also projects itself emotionally into our lives.

The figures are not exact casts but approximate ones, and they are not casts in the traditional sense, since they are made outside the negative mould, rather than from within. Segal composes his works through drawings, plans, and studies of movement, colour and gesture. As he applies cheesecloth soaked in wet plaster to the live models, he works the surface texturally, using only his hands; the casts have a roughened, expressionist surface. After the plaster is dry he makes adjustments, and since he casts in sections he can rectify or modify his proportions and shapes subtly in the mating of the pieces, without changing the basic design. He says, 'There are so many choices possible – I have to give it a nudge in this direction or that.'

His first sculpture was made in 1958, and it may have been connected to a Happening that Allan Kaprow arranged on Segal's New Jersey chicken farm the same year. At that time, he says, the problem was to grasp a 'true pictorial space'. He was not content with academic solutions and was determined to penetrate into real space. The Happening indicated the way, with its transitory action, and its spontaneous, unplanned movements. Since then, although he has been directly involved with Happenings, Segal now refuses to make them because he says his art needs contemplation.

A Native New Yorker, he was born in 1926 and taught drawing after graduating from New York University and earning his master's degree at Rutgers. He first showed his paintings in 1955. As a student of Hans Hofmann he became familiar with the teacher's abstract principles, but painted biblical and allegorical figure subjects. His first work cast from a living body was *Man at a Table* in 1961. It was done 'as a kind of Dada joke: a ready-made person at a ready-made table.' But these ironic, almost accidental 'sculptures' turned into a serious investigation of the possibilities of such form.

Segal's works, strangely enough, seem to relate more to painting than to sculpture. They are set in an imaginary boxed area of space, like a shop window display, and often one feels an imaginary picture-plane superimposed in front of his groups. A painting aesthetic in three dimensions is realised, if such a thing is possible.

The figures in dead-white plaster paradoxically seem more alive than the real objects among them. Is it possible that without any traditional illusory means such as colour or finish, his frankly synthetic humans can appear more real than reality? On the other hand, Barbara Rose finds, 'Segal's "mummies" are a page from our own Book of the Dead.'

Segal himself feels his works 'raise questions about the nature of the real object, and of relationships between human beings. Four people on a bus – how do they relate to each other? It's no accident that the subject matter of so called New Realism is concerned with the intimacy of daily life – your relationship to the food on your breakfast table and to the woman across the table.'

GEORGE SEGAL: CINEMA, 1963. *Plaster figure, illuminated plexiglas, metal sign, life-size. Collection Albright-Knox Art Gallery, gift of Mr Seymour H. Knox.*

TOM WESSELMANN: THREE-D DRAWING FOR STILL LIFE 42, 1964. *Charcoal drawn and real objects, 4′ × 5′ × 8″ depth. Collection James A. Michener Foundation. Courtesy Green Gallery, New York.*

ANDY WARHOL: CAMPBELL SOUP CAN, 1964. *Silk screen on canvas, 35¾″ × 24″. Courtesy Leo Castelli Gallery, New York.*

ANDY WARHOL: JACKIE, 1964. *Silk screen on canvas, 20" × 16". Courtesy Leo Castelli Gallery, New York.*

ANDY WARHOL

Of all the New Super Realists, Andy Warhol is the most straightforward, and forces the issue of mechanical versus hand-made almost to the breaking point. His pictures allow little give and take: you either accept them as art or you don't; there is nothing in between. He avoids any reference to painting, either of the past or present, and he not only uses mechanical processes but even has assistants who do the work for him, thus removing us as far as possible from a fine art experience.

If, as it has been suggested, Abstract Expressionists have reduced to a minimum the difference between creator and creation, and Pop has reduced to a minimum the difference between ready-made and hand-made, then Warhol must be the new movement's perfect exponent.

Silk-screening photographic news images, or stencilling commercial labels in a sort of orgasm of aesthetic 'delight', Warhol and his assistants turn out dozens of the same object, whether exact stencil replicas of *Brillo* crates which ironically were designed by Abstract Expressionist Jim Harvey (in solid and unfunctional form) or signed, real Campbell Soup tins. The silk screening and stencilling is done in varying sizes and degrees of intensity, and slight variations can occur from image to image. But these series of never-ending candid photos and brand labels run through our minds with a terrifying monotony that forces us to concentrate on the most minute changes in density, positioning and detail. Both High Camp and emotional *ennui* seem to be expressed in these forced experiences of pleasure in repetition; it is as if we were seeing a reflection of a feeling at the end of a camera lens.

One can find in Warhol's subject matter much to moralise upon, although this is certainly not a stated intention: Negro-hunts in Alabama, a waiting electric chair, Jackie Kennedy's horror-stricken face, Marilyn Monroe trapped in her own gilt-edged image, the 'Disaster' series of deaths. But nothing is overtly stated except by repetition, and we are thrown into a confusion between reading the images in strip form as a 'message' and appreciating the formal design effects for their own sake.

Some see Warhol as a great *faux naif* in the tradition of Douanier Rousseau (who also never objected to someone finishing his paintings). Others consider him a supra-intellectual, and still others think of him as a brilliant art director, organising his images with the timeliness and insight of a window display man.

Warhol himself wants to be a machine: 'The things I want to show are mechanical. Machines have less problems.' He further clarifies his position by stating, 'I think somebody should be able to do all my paintings for me. I think it would be so great if more people took up silk screens so that no one would know whether my picture was mine or somebody else's.' He predicts, 'Some day everybody will think just what they want to think, and then everybody will probably be thinking alike.'

He was born in Pittsburgh and started his career as commercial artist, doing shoe advertisements, greeting cards and window displays. His blown-up comic strip paintings of Dick Tracy were used as a 1961 window display for Lord and Taylor's. It is rumoured that he 'painted' his first stencil pictures of dollar bills around 1961 on the suggestion of a lady art dealer; when she asked him what was the most important thing in his life, his answer was, 'Money'. 'Well, then', she reputedly advised, 'paint it!' He began his Campbell Soup tin 'paintings' because 'I used to drink it. I used to have the same lunch every day, for twenty years, I guess; the same thing over and over again.'

Boredom holds a particular fascination for Warhol, and he has experimented with the lengths to which one can go and still retain some thread of interest: like a gramophone needle stuck in a groove, the same thing repeats over and over, until it begins to assume a new rhythm and pattern of its own. In his experimental films he deals with subjects that test our ability to hold attention fixed on one image without shift in focus, angle or distance, for almost unendurable lengths of time. *Sleep* has a camera trained on a man sleeping for over six hours, *Empire* scrutinizes one façade of the Empire State Building for eight, and *Henry Geldzahler* shows a close-up of the Metropolitan Museum official smoking a cigar for ninety minutes. The magazine *Film Culture* finds in these films that 'The world becomes transposed, intensified, electrified. We see it sharper than before . . . as pure as it is in itself; eating as eating, sleeping as sleeping, haircut as haircut.'

Warhol's answers to questions by Geldzahler perhaps throw some light on his unique point of view about his art:

Geldzahler: Do you know what you are doing?

Warhol: No.
Geldzahler: Do you know what a 'painting' is going to look like before you do it?
Warhol: Yes.
Geldzahler: Does it end up looking like you expect?
Warhol: No.
Geldzahler: Are you surprised?
Warhol: No.

Tom Wesselmann has, perhaps, taken most seriously Rauschenberg's example of acting in the 'gap' between art and life. He is investigating on his own terms the purgatory between illusion and reality: a real ice-box, a painted pot of flowers on top, a painted nude, a photographic montage indicating an interior, a reproduction of a Renoir next to a Miss America beauty, a full blast television, a blaring radio, his own version of a still life by Cézanne and a real telephone which rings. (At the opening of one of his shows, a visitor was heard to say: 'Won't somebody please answer that picture?')

Such juxtapositions create a number of sudden and unexpected shifts between the 'real' world and the world of 'art'. Painted areas, reproduced surfaces, and real objects are all competing for our attention and inviting us to adjust our methods of receiving visual messages within one aesthetic framework. With all elements in a state of transition, there is no pre-determined condition of medium or technique and one is in a constantly changing aesthetic focus.

Wesselmann's art seems the most theoretical and often sinks under the weight of its own content, but philosophically he is one of the most interesting in the movement, and the questions his works pose, such as what is ugly and what is beautiful, are undeniably compelling. Interviewed by Swenson, he said that the cigarette ad and the painted apple are two different realities which trade on each other: 'Lots of things – bright, strong colours, the qualities of materials, images from art history or advertising – trade on each other. This kind of relationship helps establish a momentum through the picture.' He claims that 'painting relates to both beauty and ugliness. Neither can be made (I try to work in the gap between the two).'

Advertising images excite him 'mainly because of what I can make from them. Also I use real objects because I need to use real objects, not because objects need to be used.' Moreover, he believes firmly that 'all painting is fact, and that is enough;

the paintings are charged with their very [own] presence. The situation, physical ideas, physical presence – I feel that is the comment.'

Although he works in three dimensions and 'high relief', his works are not, strictly speaking, Environments, because they retain the space of a flat painting, and do not necessarily invite one to become physically involved in them.

Born in Cincinnati, Ohio, in 1931, he graduated from the Art Academy in 1956, and came to New York. He entered Cooper Union School of Art in 1955, a year after he had his first show, shared with Jim Dine at the Judson Gallery. In late 1961 the Tanager Gallery, one of the more important Tenth Street galleries, showed his work, and the next year he was included in the Museum of Modern Art's *Recent Painting USA: The Figure* and in the *New Realist* exhibition at the Sidney Janis Gallery, which brought to the surface the gathering force of New Super Realism.

Of all the young artists, he is the most impressed by de Kooning, and he admits, 'I use de Kooning's brush knowing it is his brush.' But his flatly painted nudes recall Matisse as they lie or stand in sharp outline against their over-defined real backgrounds; and often the painted nude, because of her sensuous, artistic rendering, becomes more real than the real bathroom fixture she is seen against.

Wesselmann's latest works have assumed a purity of line and colour, and he has in some cases restricted himself either to fewer combined objects or to a narrower range of tone. He has also used moulded plastic with coloured printed images, lit from behind like a grocery store display sign. His series of 3-D 'drawings' in black and white charcoal, in which backgrounds as well as objects are 'drawn' upon, strike one as being almost traditional.

Great Britain

Although he is preoccupied mainly with the popular idols of both past and present, Peter Blake does not feel it is necessary to render them in their own ad-mass style; he is not interested in commercial techniques, or idioms, or in the allusions to the jazzy, jivey, supercharged style of the Hollywood Show-Biz world he so enjoys illustrating.

Blake is a painter in the traditional sense, and not without a degree of both nostalgia and sentimentalism as befits his English heritage: Brighton funfair life, penny arcades, postcards, shooting galleries, followed by movie stars, prize fight heroes, pop singers, circus artistes – all done in a painterly manner.

His work leaves no doubt that he indirectly uses popular sources of imagery for inspiration, and when commissioned to do *Essex in Ireland* for Richard Buckle's Shakespeare Exhibition in 1964, he told him: 'It doesn't matter whether I know the history, or even what Essex really looked like. I saw the film with Errol Flynn.' But at the same time he is not against going straight to the model, and he once remarked to David Sylvester that 'the Beatles aren't available. Ideally I'd paint their portraits.' Instead he used their photos for his painting. If he uses record sleeves, fan magazine snaphots, posters, etc. to depict his popular heroes, he makes no direct reference to the source of his visual information, but paints as if he were working directly from reality.

David Sylvester feels that Blake's work is based on a folk art style, such as that of inn signs and circus posters, but lettering apart (and the stencil-legend is usually an essential part of his design) the approach seems closer to traditional English Royal Academy painting, with a delicate touch, a tentative handling of *matière* and a strong sense of drawing. In fact, he showed at the R.A. in 1965.

Since his trip to California in 1964 to fulfil a magazine commission in which he was asked to record the place with which he most felt an affinity, his style has opened up and become more relaxed and sprawling. Perhaps like Californian life itself, with its wide streets, its motorised existence, bright colours, fantasy restaurants shaped like a 'donut' or a Derby hat, and its playground atmosphere, Blake has not only examined first hand the well-spring of his inspiration, but has found a more natural response to it.

It is understandable that an English artist might fall in love with the American Dream as experienced from afar, through movies and glossy magazines, but Blake's trip to Hollywood has given him an opportunity to sketch directly a world he obviously responds to emotionally as well as visually. He remains an outsider, as he must, always looking in, summing up, editing, or indirectly commenting on what he has found in the 'Golden West', but his point of view is sympathetic and descriptive, rather than critical.

In his earlier work going back to 1954, Blake dealt more directly with the nostalgic trappings of popular culture: the picture postcards, the pin-ups, the old medals and sports trophies, targets, hearts, comic-strips (he used one in 1957), and magazine photographs, rich in associations. Pinned to some piece of architecture, say, a door or a wall, they seem more like found images than organized and arranged ones. *The Girl Door* or *The Love Wall*, crowded with postcards and photographs, remind us of the possibilities Eluard saw in the postcard years ago, when he wrote: 'Commissioned by the exploiters to amuse the exploited, they should not, however, be counted a popular art. They are, rather, the small change of art and of poetry: and this small change sometimes reveals ideas of gold.'

But Blake himself might not agree: 'What I'm doing becomes folk art', he insists, and among all the New Super Realists, he prides himself on painting for the non-specialist. For instance, he was extremely pleased that *The Da Vinci Brothers* (two professional wrestlers called Sir Conrad and Ricky) was bought by a professional soccer player.

Born in Dartford, England, in 1932, Blake went to the Royal College of Art in 1953 and remained until 1956. He was there the same time as Dick Smith, and the two artists shared a studio for some time. The fact of their presence at the R.C.A. together may have been intellectually stimulating to the younger group of artists there around 1960. Earning a Leverhulme Travelling Scholarship, Blake spent his time studying the popular arts in the various places to which he went. His first important exhibition was at the Institute of Contemporary Arts in 1958, and he appeared for the first time in New York at the Janis Gallery's *New Realists* exhibition in 1962.

His large-scale commissions for the Shakespeare Exhibition, which in itself constituted a sort of Pop environment show, are his most ambitious works and among the biggest commissioned works of that type in England. In his version of Essex and Elizabeth, Blake's mammoth tryptich includes the *Siege of Ostend*, *The Essex Revolt*, *Essex in Ireland*, and *Drake's Last Voyage and Death*. Not since the nineteenth century *grandes machines* has history painting been tackled in such a size and with such breadth and vigour. Done in a semi-impressionist style with references to portraits and personalities, Blake used a contemporary 'Technicolor' palette and bordered the works with stripes of fairground colours, as well as stencil-legends reminiscent of billboard lettering.

There is a Victorian element about Blake's work, filled as it is with memorabilia, rich in association and scrap-book mementoes, and of all the English Pop-ists he is certainly the most unabashedly romantic. The future may find him the most evocative and nostalgic (as nostalgic as Burne-Jones or Rossetti today) of all his contemporaries.

PETER BLAKE: BO DIDDLEY, 1964/5. *Cryla on board, 48″ × 30″. Courtesy Robert Fraser Gallery, London.*

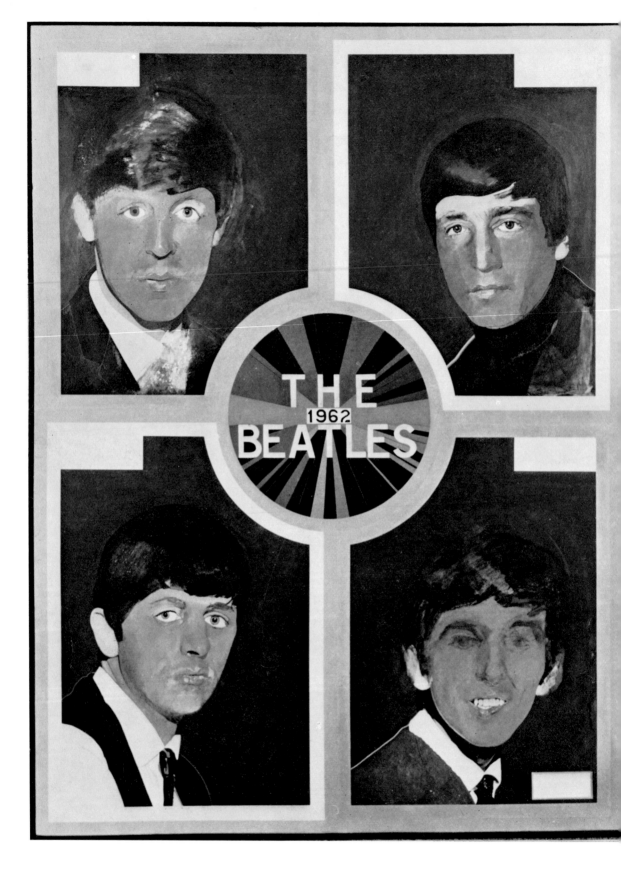

PETER BLAKE: THE BEATLES, 1964. *Oil on board, 48" × 36".*
Courtesy Robert Fraser Gallery, London.

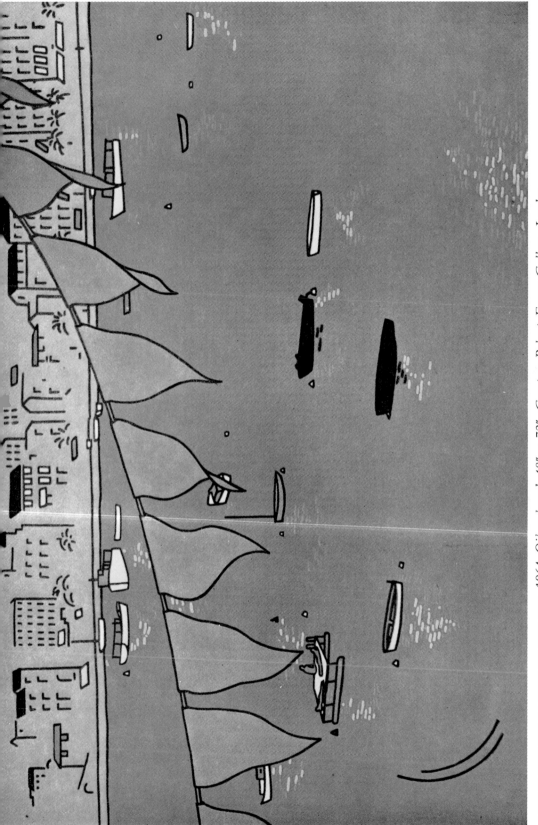

PATRICK CAULFIELD: VIEW OF THE BAY, 1964. Oil on board, 48" × 72". Courtesy Robert Fraser Gallery, London.

114

PATRICK CAULFIELD: STILL LIFE ON TABLE, 1964. *Oil on board, 48″ × 60″. Courtesy Robert Fraser Gallery, London.*

The absolute inflexibility of Patrick Caulfield's pictorial *clichés* often seem like intellectual exercises in taste in art history; they demand a high level of sophistication on the part of the viewer, despite their vulgarised subject matter.

He blatantly and unemotionally states such visual facts as they might appear in a 'paint your own picture' with numbers; on a jig-saw puzzle; stencilled on a plastic tray; embroidered on a tea towel; depicted on a luggage travel sticker; or as a Decal decoration on a kitchen cabinet.

To compare the work of Caulfield with Lichtenstein as some have done, is to misunderstand both, for although both artists delve into the depths of the banal, there is a total difference in attitude. Lichtenstein uses the basest source of illustration which has absolutely no pretence of being 'art' or 'artistic' (with the exception of the Picasso pictures) and transforms such material into an 'art experience'; Caulfield on the other hand, uses the debased illustration in an attempt to come to terms with areas of popular art that have pretentions of being fine art – the end of the road of figuration, ironed out, machine-tooled, and vulgarised beyond endurance. Thus, he is not just content to show a flattened flight of dime-store china ducks, but he must set them against a renovated 'Mondrian' abstraction as it has been translated into a wallpaper design or a decal transfer.

There is little sensuality in Caulfield (such as in Lichtenstein) and he never tries to find the beautiful in his prototypes as the American does. In fact, he keeps us strapped to the original while we witness a callous exploitation of devalued art experiences as they have come down to us after a quarter-century of crude commercial re-interpretation.

As John Russell has noticed, 'Caulfield criticises, by implication, a society which acquiesces in the mass-production of images like those available for a dollar or two in the "picture" department of multiple stores, but he is pre-eminently a historian who sets himself to discover just how far a great tradition has sunk'.

115

As Caulfield makes his forays into the no-man's land between 'good' and 'bad' taste, he does not appear to want to return the cheap and bastardised back to art, but to leave them where they are, merely clarified and pointed up. Such strange, cerebral investigations into ugliness, forced by the artist's tough attitude, push these images from one area of subconscious acceptance into another of conscious understanding, and through shifts of strengthened design and colour we see these banalities as new experiences.

The thickness of Caulfield's line, which is even and unvaried, the flat harshness of the colour, the total lack of space in the composition, do not even leave us with an area of feeling in which to take refuge; such a manner produces so unemotional an effect, that Lichtenstein seems highly expressive by comparison.

David Thompson finds in Caulfield's works that the 'best paintings often have the same disconcerting effect as the sort of high-minded *cliché* that stops discussion dead in its tracks ... with a deadpan seriousness of manner which is as remote from sentimentality as it is from humourous indulgence.'

Born in London in 1936, Caulfield studied at the Chelsea School of Art from 1957 to 1960, and then at the Royal College of Art from 1960 to 1963. He travelled in Italy and France in 1961 and again in 1963, and has had major exhibitions in London, at the Robert Fraser Gallery, and in New York.

One of the most unyielding of all the New Super Realists, Caulfield is closer to the American aesthetic than most of his compatriots in so far as he is totally removed from direct comment or involvement (except through choice of subject), and he presents his images in such a poker-faced manner that we are left wondering what sort of reaction we are meant to have. In fact, even Americans find his hard-edge impersonal imagery very difficult to take.

Although too eccentric an artist to be considered strictly New Super Realist, David Hockney has his place in the movement partly through subject matter gleaned from physical culture illustration, partly through his delightful sense of Camp, and partly through a detached social-satirical attitude expressed in the most glib terms of the *faux naïf*.

Like Lichtenstein, Hockney uses a low form of illustration, in this case the child's cartoon caricature. But he is consciously folksy or whimsical in his drawing, and eschews the supra-sophisticated ad-mass style for a sort of untrained 'art' that appears deceptively casual.

His California series and his Domestic Interiors, although taken to a large degree from muscle magazine drawings and photographs, are not transcribed directly or even scrutinised methodically. Instead, he allows himself freedom to range over a wide area of abstract form and line while he transforms his popular subjects into something highly personal.

Like many of the New Super Realists, he insists that before he tackles the subjects he begins with a 'pure' aesthetic, and that his basic considerations are formal, abstract ones – the same that he has been dealing with since 1961.

Hockney's brand of naiveté, so reminiscent of the earlier work of Andy Warhol, is achieved through his deliberately 'ugly' or awkward drawing, always kept in exquisite control. Moreover, trappings such as cheap floral cretonnes, shower-plumbing, potted plants, pelmet boards and over-stuffed furniture, are handled with a shrewd perception, and we constantly wonder whether he is enjoying what he observes with an innocent eye, or whether he is deliberately 'sending it up'.

His imaginative, exotic settings, such as the Egyptian scenes done before and after he went to the Middle East in 1963, have a sort of romantic glamour, not unlike the travel ads that try to lure us to far-off places which we know will never be as they are portrayed.

In his Domestic Interiors, he hits out the hardest. Here is a strange magazine world of ageing physical culture 'youths' living vapid lives under stall showers, or in slip-covered armchairs in narcissistic nudity. Semi-bald, with stupid faces, they appear mechanised and without souls. All of them have curtains to stand in front of, to hide behind or just to decorate dreary lives. With less than two decades to 1984, Hockney's wry depictions of these sexless mass-think creatures hint broadly that we may already be there.

The ever-present oblique social comment in Hockney's whimsical work becomes most poignant in *The Rake's Progress*, a series of etchings. Done partly in London, but mostly in and around New York, they truly reflect the artist's own reactions to the Brave New World he faced on his first visit to the United States in 1961. The *Drinking Scene* is a Bowery bar with weeping men; the *Death* is a garish, gaping coffin in Harlem; the *Gospel Singing Good People* is a Madison Square Garden rally, attended by an audience of striped neckties announcing 'God is Love.' One of the wittiest is the *Bedlam Scene*, depicting a row of automata marching backward to their own music, which comes from ingrown pocket transistor radios; to proclaim their faith in the drug of canned music, their tee shirts announce: 'I Swing with W.A.B.C.' (a commercial radio station).

These etchings have little to do with Hogarth, despite their title, except that they come from the same English fondness for social satire. They are related more to the inventive freedom of style in the traditional English lampoon-caricature, which goes back to Rowlandson, Gillray, Spy and others. Thus, Hockney seems to have returned to a type of satire which Lawrence Alloway considered the first truly popular art, since such eighteenth century published cartoons were printed in large editions, sold cheaply, and circulated freely as commonly understood and accepted property.

Hockney is, like the Beatles, either a 'natural' or a highly sophisticated artist who is perfectly aware of the Camp quality in his work. Both possibilities are evident, but one is never sure what is irony, and what is done straight, out of genuine feeling.

Born in Bradford, Yorkshire, in 1937, Hockney attended the Bradford College of Art, was a conscientious objector from 1957 to 1959, and then attended the Royal College of Art for four years. His work first appeared in the Young Contemporaries Exhibition of 1961, after which he left for New York. He returned to New York in the Spring of 1963 to finish the *Rake's Progress* and at the end of the year went to Los Angeles, California for a year. He prefers the West Coast with its bizarre, exaggerated, out-of-scale existence and has taught painting there on and off, but he also loves the 'popular' culture life of Forty-second Street, with its sexy movie houses, its novelty shops selling outlandish party tricks and its raffish, cheap glitter.

DAVID HOCKNEY: TYPHOO TEA 1960. *Oil on canvas, 54" × 36". Courtesy Kasmin Gallery, London.*

DAVID HOCKNEY: MAN TAKING A SHOWER IN BEVERLY HILLS, 1964. *Acrylic on canvas, 65½″ × 65½″. Collection, The Arbams Family New York. Courtesy the Alan Gallery, New York.*

GERALD LAING: SKY DIVER VII, 1964. *Oil on canvas, 84″ × 60¾″. Courtesy Richard Feigen Gallery, New York.*

ALLEN JONES: BUSES, 1964. *Oil on canvas, 108″ × 120″. Courtesy of Arthur Tooth and Sons, London. Collection The Stuyvesant Foundation.*

Hockney's second Typhoo tea box, *Painting in the Illusionistic Style*, begun in 1961 and shown the following year at the Young Contemporaries, was the first 'shaped' canvas of the new art in Britain. The cut out pieces were attached together to form the outline of a tea box in a sort of rough three-dimensional perspective. Although he has since left the shaped canvas, he still deals with his own kind of flat-plane 'illusion', by means of a shallow space and a rude perspective.

The gaiety, affability and exhilarating freedom from moralising in the New Super Realism seems best combined in the work of Allen Jones.

He is one of the most decorative and light-hearted of the Pop-ists, and a bright, fun-loving quality pervades his work; yet, easy as it appears to be, there is a sardonic punch in its sex imagery, which includes flamboyant girlie pix, legs, garters, undies, loud neckties, and overblown cleavages.

Instead of hard, factual mass-media images, served straight, Jones stays within the European tradition of 'fine art' colour-design that goes back to the Fauves. He says he was initially inspired by Delaunay, but there is that feeling for planes of flat colour and blocked-in areas that is reminiscent of Matisse's later work. His space is purposely confusing and inconsistent, shifting from flat two-dimensional areas of tone to three-dimensional Cubist depth. These shifts of space are particularly remarkable in his Aeroplane and Bus pictures and in the series of Hermaphrodites.

Jones insists that his subject matter is the least important aspect of his work: 'It begins as a formal picture and that leads me to the imagery. The shapes themselves suggest the subject, not the subject the shapes.'

But certain subjects continually re-appear and there is a strong affection for what might be considered by some to be the cheap, meretricious, sleazy sexiness of the stripper or the pin-up. Yet, in his hands, such 'forbidden' subjects (culled from magazines) suddenly seem pleasureful, sinless and full of wit and charm. Nevertheless they still have the power to shock, and often people have read into his works obscenities which were never intended, and which the artist himself cannot see.

An admirer of Kandinsky, Jones uses 'automatic' drawing to release himself from faithfulness to the motif, even though the motif comes not from life but from second-hand magazine material. The formal ideas in his works have developed consistently and he says he is still working on the basic shaped canvas problems that occurred in his first pictures in 1961. Thus, an early self-portrait head/neck shape turned into a flower/stem idea, and has been the basis of the first shaped canvas Bus picture, ('It had to be a bus; when I finished the abstract problem, it looked just like one.'). When he found that the Bus caused more attention than the way it was painted, he turned the image upside down to flaunt its content. While working on it, 'It suddenly suggested an aeroplane cockpit.' The camouflage design that sometimes encircles his planes was observed from nature: 'Flying over a cloud once, I looked down and saw a series of concentric rainbow circles in the plane's shadows, so I painted it.' The rainbow and falling parachutist followed, and again Jones sees a direct link to earlier themes with the circle and an attached figure below. The Marriage Medals of 1963 continue this theme, with a separate, long rectangular canvas depending from an octagonal-shaped canvas.

But whether the imagery or the formal design comes first, there is an exciting tension in Jones's work between what is recognizable and what is pure design: do we see a striped necktie or a riband of colours? Is it a pair of ladies' panties, or a clear field of blue floating in space? Is it a traffic jam in Trafalgar Square, or a patchwork of bright squares pushing each other across the canvas from right to left? Such interchanges between recognized and abstracted form create a delightful visual puzzle.

Born in Southampton in 1937, Jones studied at the Hornsey College of Art in 1958 and 1959, and then moved to the Royal College. The Young Contemporaries Exhibition of 1961 brought him public attention, and it is worth noticing that he was secretary of that now historical event. After the show, he was commissioned by Courtaulds to do a large mural for the staff dining room, which was later considered too obscene to hang, although the artist himself was mystified as to what obscenity it represented. He won the *Prix de Jeunes Artistes* at the Paris Biennale in 1963, has had major one-man shows in London and New York, and has lived in New York.

The big city, particularly New York, is for him an unreal place, which makes its own myths into extraordinary realities. He constantly 'wonders' over the new imagery it provides, but although he may spend time in the trick-game shops on Broadway, and even come home with a pair of 'Party Falsies' ('*For Gals (and Guys)*: *WOW*'), he strongly denies that such things are central to the imagery in his work; they are considered merely as peripheral boosts to his visual imagination. *Playboy* is to a large degree a source of material, as are other slick, sexy magazines, inspiring him to use an almost tongue-in-cheek attitude to modern mass-culture sex-symbolism. Today's confusion between male and female, so strongly felt in wearing apparel and sexual attitudes, is implicitly expressed in his *Hermaphrodites*, who are not so much the sex-change type or the transvestite, as ambiguous half-male, half-female figures, who change wilfully back and forth, while retaining the essential properties of both.

GERALD LAING

Considering the magazine and news photograph as one of the most important sources of contemporary imagery in our time, Gerald Laing has restricted himself to working with such published pictures as capture his imagination. His two favourite subjects are bathing beauties in bikinis and 'dragster' motor racers.

He converts his chosen themes into paintings by means of a careful rendition of the half-tone screen of dots with which photos are printed, but his technique does not make use of the mechanical, as Lichtenstein's the Ben Day screen, or Phillips's the air-brush gun. Laing is fascinated by the craftmanship involved in building up his forms with hand-painted dots in a style which approximates a more regulated type of monochrome Pointillism. Comparison with the original photograph confirms that there is a very wide range of freedom employed within the photographic half-tone convention and that Laing's 'dot' system is completely made up: instead of building the images with white dots on black that move through black dots on white, there is a looser patterning on an all-white background, in which the white solids are lost in the white canvas while the black dots define the forms. As painstaking as such a method is, he enjoys doing the dots himself: 'It's like knitting.' One might say that Laing's subjects are schematised from the prototype into semi-abstractions, which recall, either more or less, some shadow of the original image.

He feels that both the overdressed 'dragster' get-up of crash helmet and racing cover-all, and the underdressed bikini 'uniform', equally reduce the subjects inside to a standardised stereotype: 'Every model girl's belly button looks pretty much the same.'

His 'dragsters' provide a somewhat more complicated iconography than his girls, not only by virtue of the breadth of formal design they allow, but by their own peculiar fetishist nature. Laing is himself passionately interested in racing cars and he finds something particularly fascinating about the 'souped up' machine which has been added to, subtracted from, reformed, changed, and super-charged to the point where

GERALD LAING: AA-D, 1964. *Oil on canvas, 55" × 83".*
Collection Mr John G. Powers, New Jersey. 127

PETER PHILLIPS: STAR PLAYERS, 1962. *Drawing, 23" × 18".*
Collection Mr Peter Cochran, London.

it has lost its former use and is only fit for a six-second straight run (it cannot even turn) at 200 m.p.h.: 'It's faster than a rocket; in fact, so fast that it cannot even stop itself easily, and an attached parachute must be opened to slow it down.'

Here the mechanical or mass produced object is transformed into a work of art (rather than the other way round) since its functional aspect has been so narrowed that Laing feels it 'almost becomes a piece of elaborate sculpture on wheels.'

Such a subject, discovered in racing annuals and sports magazines, is a strong stimulus to his work: 'It has to be. I couldn't get through a painting unless it interested me.' But it is not the major factor involved.

Laing was born in Newcastle-Upon-Tyne in 1936, and attended Sandhurst when he was 18 for two years; he did five years' service as a professional soldier. In 1960 he left his army career to join the St. Martin's School of Art, where Dick Smith taught around 1962. Smith became a strong influence in opening up possibilities that Laing had never considered before. He says he began his dots at school as a sort of joke, to see if he could really bring it off on a large scale, but soon he became so interested with the problems of building form in this way that he concentrated his efforts on developing his own system.

When Laing first came to New York in the summer of 1963, he knew Robert Indiana and was much impressed by the American's cool, hard-edge brilliance. He wanted to approximate the same sort of feeling but in his own terms. Thus, he restricted his colour to an occasional letter or a stripe of Day-Glo red or green, to set off the stark black and white dot images enlarged to enormous proportions, sometimes on a 'shaped' canvas, sometimes within the traditional rectangle. He was given his first exhibition in New York, at the Feigen Gallery in 1964, before his work was even seen in his native England.

He declares his major influence to be Paolo Uccello, since the early Renaissance master was equally interested in schematic depictions of human figures, and what Laing refers to as 'styling': 'After all, Uccello's figures were always in the latest fashion.' He considers both fashion and styling important elements of art, and he wants a picture done in 1965 to look 'very '65.'

And yet certain other formal stylisations are evident in his work, perhaps due more to what he sees in the original photograph than to any conscious reference to art history. For instance, the forms and lines of his opened parachutes, blossoming behind his front-on racers take on an abstracted Art Nouveau air, sinewy and full of curves, and somehow extremely synthetic.

With Peter Phillips, Laing engineered *Hybrid* in New York in 1965. A consumer research work of art, its component parts were made up of an 'average' chosen by a number of people at random, from shapes, textures, materials and colours, out of which were put together by the two artists a computed construction that both hoped would be 'typically '65.'

PETER PHILLIPS

Among the English New Super Realists Peter Phillips is the most directly inspired by the mechanical. Since he began his art career as a student of technical draughting (he gave up when he found he was hopeless at mathematics and couldn't use a slide rule), such drawing techniques, as well as earlier training in commercial art – posters, sign-writing and silver-smithing – strongly affected the subsequent development of his style. 'My teachers in Birmingham were still using the old fashioned techniques of the 'thirties, and that is what we were taught. Everything was done very carefully on a minute scale.'

Born in Birmingham in 1939, and a student at the College of Art there from 1955 to 1959, Phillips travelled in France and Italy before enrolling at the Royal College of Art's painting and T.V. school in 1959. He flirted briefly with Abstract Expressionism, but he insists, 'I have always preferred the neat, clear-cut image. I have never liked drips – they don't appeal to me. And the sort of sensuousness in Abstract Expressionism was never really me, either.'

He therefore began taking images from second-hand sources, such as *Life, Post, Hot Rod Yearbook, Scientific American, Playboy*, etc., around 1960. The following year, as President of the Young Contemporaries exhibition in London, he organised the first showing of the works of fellow students, Allen Jones, David Hockney, Derek Boshier and Ron Kitaj. He says the American, Kitaj, an older colleague at the school, was most influential in showing the English students an *attitude* toward painting that gave them more freedom with both technique and subject matter.

Phillips's girlie images, which are always inextricably worked into obsessively careful depictions of car parts, motorbikes, mechanical objects, carburettors, heaters, bumpers, fans or dashboards, look on the face of it like old-fashioned pin-ups of the 1940's, and at least one critic finds them 'nostalgic'. However, it is clear from today's girlie magazines that the pin-ups Phillips uses are just as current now as they were in the 'forties; and although specifically a war-time pin-up, the *Esquire* Vargas girl in, say, his *Gravy for the Navy* is identical with those cliché models that air brush artists such as Hubenthal and Petty use today in sexy magazines. But it is less the subject that interests Phillips than the technique employed, for as he puts it: 'Technique can be an aesthetic just as much as subject or anything else.'

Phillips borrows directly from the work of the unsuspecting air brush artist who produces precisely-modelled nudes or motor parts with the same impersonal evenness of tone and texture: 'These people are wonderful artists technically, and they offer a lot.' One of the most important changes in Phillips's work since his stay in New York in 1964/65 was his use of the air brush gun, and only small areas of his canvases were hand painted at this time. He feels this switch to a machine has been a major improvement, since he had always attempted to produce the finish and perfection of the machine-rendered; but the brush-work, no matter how careful, would get in the way. 'I don't want to be a machine like Warhol,' he says, 'but I love the idea of using one.'

Phillips has remained basically European in his sense of space-composition. Unlike Americans who open up their canvases, he uses a crowded space, exquisitely organised and carefully manipulated so that it can easily contain the many objects he integrates into a formal pattern.

David Thompson finds that Phillips 'has most consistently kept . . . [Pop's] original tone. The images he assembles retain the brashness and stridency of their authentic urban-entertainment context . . . But what is peculiar to him is the slight undercurrent of menace or violence, the lack of innocence, in this hectic pursuit of pleasure.'

But the sinister elements that some find in Phillips's 'S and M' black-bordered paintings of motorbikes, crash helmets and leather kit is part projection, since the artist himself claims: 'My crash helmets and motorcycles are not "kinky"; I use them for different ends than just fetishism. The imagery is not important or significant for itself; it is the way it is painted and used that matters.' The content is useful for the visual excitement it induced originally in the artist, and for the formal way it can be utilised in terms of the composition.

RICHARD SMITH: VISTA, 1963. *Oil on canvas, 60" × 84". Courtesy Kasmin Gallery, London.*

133

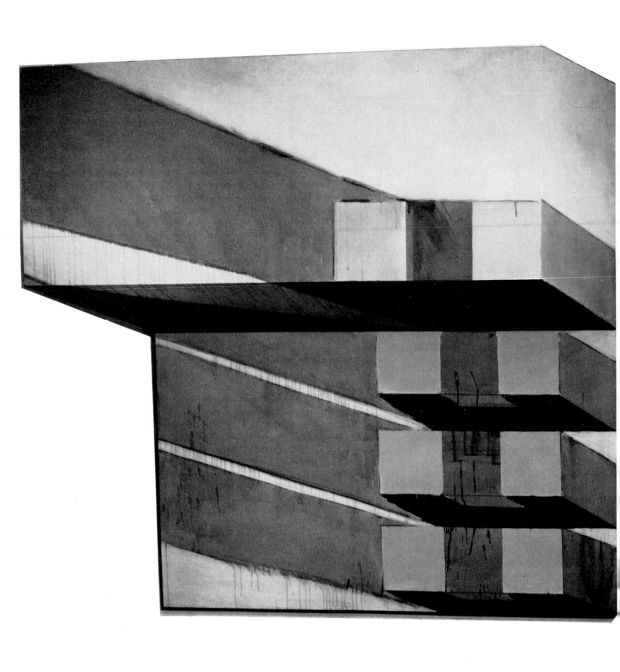

RICHARD SMITH: QUARTET, 1964. *Acrylic on canvas, 56″ × 72″ × 20½″. Collection Walker Art Center, Minneapolis. Courtesy Green Gallery, New York.*

R. B. KITAJ: THE OHIO GANG, 1964. *Oil on canvas, 72″ × 72″.*
Courtesy Marlborough-Gerson Gallery, New York.

135

R. B. KITAJ: THE NICE OLD MAN AND THE PRETTY GIRL, 1964. *Oil on canvas, 48" × 48". Courtesy Marlborough-Gerson Gallery, New York.*

Anglo-American

RICHARD SMITH

Some might disagree that Richard Smith is a New Super Realist. Yet, he is one of the most central figures in English Pop and his work is greatly admired by the younger artists of the group. His deep interest in American ways of painting, and his fascination for new means of mass-media communications, advertising, and packaging, alone might earn him a place in the new movement.

But more important, Smith's large, three-dimensional 'shaped canvases' prove the variety and complexity of the New Super Realism when it extends itself beyond just a mere technical investigation of the banal, and takes up painterly devices once more.

At first glance, Smith's work, which takes off from the wall or floor and enters the space between the picture plane and the spectator, seems to be a kind of extended sculpture-painting, on to which a sensitive skin of abstract expressionist brushwork is lovingly grafted. But closer study reveals that the shapes and forms come from commercial packaging, the boxes and cartons that surround our daily lives, and into which our very existence seems to be neatly and sterilely sorted out. It is not the specific brand-label that is in Smith's mind, but the total design element of the package which tempts him to take up where the commercial artist has left off. He uses various ad-mass devices such as 'spotlighting', the zig-zag line, or the 'zoom lens' shape, as they might appear on a box of soap flakes, a cigarette packet or a matchbook cover; but there is such a high degree of transformation that we are not quite sure whether commercial packaging reminds us of Smith's work, or whether his work reminds us of commercial packaging. Did these cartons and crates which first inspired him, initiate these later box-like structures, or is it Smith's shapes which now in retrospect suggest manufactured items?

'There is a strong formal direction,' the artist says, 'but this can be shifted; the emphasis itself can be shifted by things outside. The give and take between the two is so enmeshed that I don't know which is foremost.'

Smith admits that he no longer gets as many kicks from exterior things as he did a few years ago, but he says, 'The *Kent* cigarette advertisement is still a beautiful idea that fascinates me; that white packet on a white background is so perfect.'

He also finds the Admiral TV sign on Broadway one of the most inspiring sights, with its constant changes of patterns and shapes, throughout a repeated commercial. Other popular imagery, which may or may not be influential, and which he admires, are the neon *Canadian Club* sign on Broadway with its spinning discs of light, and the *Salem* cigarette twenties packet.

'The communication media are a large part of my landscape,' admits Smith, but he adds, 'My interest is not in the message so much as in the method.'

Born in Letchworth in 1931, Smith served with the R.A.F. from 1950–52 in Hong Kong, and then enrolled at the St. Albans School of Art. He continued his art education at the Royal College of Art in London where he studied from 1954–57. Joining the revolution against Establishment values in England which was taking place in the mid-'fifties, he knew of both Richard Hamilton's and Paolozzi's experiments with popular imagery at the I.C.A. and he himself wrote articles in *Ark* on various phases of popular culture from 1956 on. The following year, he gave a lecture at the Institute of Contemporary Arts with Roger Coleman, entitled 'Man About Mid-century' which dealt sociolgically with the changing fashions in men's clothing. *This Is Tomorrow* made a deep impression on him, and he remembers vividly the stands of both Paolozzi and Hamilton in the Whitechapel exhibition.

After teaching at Hammersmith College from 1957-58, he moved to New York for three years and was given his first show there in 1961. He now spends half his time in America.

His interest in popular culture has always been evident, but the package began to dominate his work around 1960–61: 'I had always liked boxes, but the first specific "box" painting, I suppose, was in 1962 – the reference was fairly direct, since it was a shape in perspective.'

Smith's prototype now is not the box itself, but some commercial rendition of the box such as a coloured photograph from a magazine, or a billboard painting. He did a picture called *Billboard* in 1961, along with other pictures that had specific commercial titles, like *McCalls*, and at that time he also made references to trick shutter-lenses and various kinds of slick photographic techniques.

In 1962 he made a film with Robert Freeman called *Trailer*, which examined, through the camera's eye, slices of cake, cigars, tyres, commercial packages, watches and other mass-produced items.

Among all the English Pop-ists, Smith seems the least afraid to tackle the large-scale work, and his gigantism takes the form of huge three-dimensional constructions of shaped canvases (actually moulded plywood forms covered with canvas and then painted) that attach to walls in one form or another: 'The scale of a painting is often physically related to the hoardings [billboards] or cinema screens which never present objects actual size. You could drown in a glass of beer, or live in a semi-detached cigarette pack.'

These large, half-expressionist, half-Pop images seem to have no formal limitations as they emerge from the picture plane and move into space. A paint surface, at once vigorous, yet sensitive, with highly charged colours playing against soft, subtle edges, appears to be born out of the scale and shape. Of all the English artists inspired by the American manner, Smith alone has managed a delicate balance between traditional English sensibility and the jazzy, strident, manufactured culture of New York's new world.

R. B. KITAJ

A brilliant eclectic, Ron Kitaj's painting would be difficult to categorise in any age: part history painter, part *pasticheur*, part philosopher and part Pop, all elements are combined in his work with a devastating style which almost approaches the slick; he is saved by his ability to do the unexpected at the right moment and jolt us into some new or forgotten realisation.

Often using the story-telling comic-strip style to make a point of social or political significance, he does not, however, tell his stories in sequence or in any particular frame of reference. They appear as a jumble of images, reshuffled or fragmented to suit the formal demands of the work. The result is like flipping quickly through the pages of a glossy magazine, catching only an occasional illustration, or else watching the unrelated billboards rush by from a train window. Yet, out of these disconnected shards of commercial figuration, we are somehow led to some significant point which is almost always political or literary.

His ad-mass idiom includes the modelling of the high contrast photo print, photographic tone, and requotations of already printed popular images, as well as matt paint surfaces, reminiscent of sign painting. Colours are usually direct, primary and untampered.

There is a strong connection in some of his works with Duchamp, particularly in the 'corrected' ready-mades – often nothing more than a page torn from an auction catalogue, an old photograph or the title page of a favourite book, mounted, signed and framed by him.

An intellectual with a wide and varied education, Kitaj is fond of making use of his literary and poetic knowledge in a variety of ways, and his major sources can range from Kafka, Norman Douglas, Dostoyevsky and books of the political left, to Babel, Sorel and Jonathan Williams' poetry. There is no consistent programme in his subject matter; everything and anything is used as raw material for the construction of these remarkable paintings which show a diverse use of technique, imagery and style. But certain themes, such as histories of violence, death, rebirth, and social injustice, reappear as a *leit-motif* in his work.

Born in Cleveland in 1932, Kitaj arrived at Oxford in 1957 to study art at The Ruskin School under the G.I. Bill of Rights (he was a veteran of the Korean War). He says he felt little influence of British art at this time, but had always admired the work of Eduardo Paolozzi: 'Bonnard, Matisse, and Cézanne were the artists that influenced me when I was a child.' He feels that everything in art that has happened since, has had some effect on his work.

'Who couldn't have been influenced by Abstract Expressionism? It is in all of us: Jim Dine, Rauschenberg, Johns; it is part of what we experienced and we cannot avoid it. There is no break from one to the other – it is a clear continuation.'

He feels there has been a great over-emphasis on Cubism and much under-estimation of Surrealism: 'All the Abstract Expressionists from Pollock on come from Surrealism. It is perhaps most notable in Baziotes and Gorky, but even Rothko has an element of it. More than that, every important artist of our time has been influenced by it: Klee, Ernst, Picasso.'

Kitaj's overwhelming influence on young British New Super Realists may be entirely circumstantial since he happened to be studying at the Royal College of Art from 1959 on, during a time when an outstanding group of students were there. On the other hand, Phillips, Jones and Hockney could not help being curious about how a 'real live American' painted at a time when the New York school had taken the lead over Paris.

Both Jones and Hockney remember being impressed with his work at the College, and they watched him labour with great interest; Jones says, 'He drew very carefully, with long pauses between each stroke made on the paper.' Hockney says, 'I used to see one image in the corner of his canvas and think, "that's terrific!", but when I came back the next week expecting to see the canvas filled, he would still be working on the same image.'

This American who has made London his home first appeared at the Young Contemporaries 1961 exhibition, where he was an instant success, achieving fame before his fellow students who had arranged to exhibit his work. His friendship with Paolozzi produced a joint construction which consisted of an assortment of popular images, including repeated prints of François Rude's head of Christ, which itself was done from a marble in the Louvre, a view of the New York skyline, a clock without hands, fragmented photographs, and medals of St. Louis.

When speaking of the emergence of popular imagery in art, like most other Pop-ists, Kitaj tends to minimise the content and play up the importance of design to the whole. And he says, 'There must be 2,000 possibilities for making a picture – whether formal considerations come first or last is hardly the point. In the end, the subject matter is in the artist, not in the programme. It is what the artist himself chooses that matters, rather than external things.'

An artist whose output is sporadic, and who devotes as much time to reading as to painting, he believes that 'the picture always takes over, but you can't help being moved by the great cultural issues peripheral to the picture.'

As for the chance elements that Rauschenberg is so fond of using, Kitaj says, 'Planning a picture can have just as much chance in it as not planning one.'

Selected Bibliography

ALLOWAY, LAWRENCE
'Pop Art since 1949', *The Listener*. London, December 27, 1962

BATTCOCK, GREGORY
The New Art (anthology). New York, 1966

BRETT, GUY
'Allen Jones', *The London Magazine*, IV: 2. London, May 1964

BRETT, GUY
'David Hockney, a Note in Progress', *The London Magazine*, 3: 1. London, April 1963

CAGE, JOHN
Silence, Middleton, Conn. (Wesleyan University Press), 1961

F[RANKFURTER], A[LFRED]
'Pop Extremists', *Art News*. New York, September 1964

GELDZAHLER, HENRY
'Andy Warhol', *Art International*, VIII: 3. Lugano, April 1964

JOHNSON, ELLEN H.
'The Living Object' (Claes Oldenburg), *Art International*, VII: 1. Zurich, January 1963

KAPROW, ALLAN
' "Happenings" in the New York Scene', Art News. New York, May 1961

KAPROW, ALLAN
'Segal's Vital Mummies', *Art News*. New York, February 1964

KOZLOFF, MAX
'Pop Culture, Metaphysical Disgust and the New Vulgarians', *Art International*, VI: 2. Zurich, February 1962

LEBEL, ROBERT
Marcel Duchamp. London, Paris and New York, 1959

LEVY, MERVYN
'Pop Art for Admass', *Studio* CLXI: 847. London, November 1963

LIPPARD, LUCY R.
'New York Letter 1965: Reinhardt, Duchamp, Morris', *Art International*, IX: 3, 4. 1965

LORAN, ERLE
'Pop Artists or Copy Cats', *Art News*. New York, September 1963

LYTTON, NORBERT
'American Pop Art and Richard Smith', *Art International*, VIII: 1. Lugano, February 1964

McLUHAN, MARSHALL
Understanding Media: *The Extensions of Man*. New York, 1964

MELVILLE, ROBERT
'The Durable Expendables of Peter Blake', *Motif* 10. London, Winter 1962/3

MEYER, LEONARD B.
'The End of the Renaissance?', *The Hudson Review*, XVL: 2. New York, Summer 1963

MUSEUM OF MODERN ART, NEW YORK
'Pop Art Symposium at the Museum of Modern Art', December 1962. Reprint *Arts Magazine* 1963

READ, SIR HERBERT
'Disintegration of Form in Modern Art', *Studio International*. London, April 1965

REICHARDT, JASIA
'Pop Art and After', *Art International*, VII: 2. Zurich, February 1963
RESTANY, PIERRE
'New Realism', *Art in America*, 1. New York, February 1963
REYNER BANHAM, PETER
'Who is this "Pop" ', *Motif* 10. London, Winter 1962
ROSE, BARBARA
'Dada Then and Now', *Art International*, VII: 1. Zurich, January 1963
ROSE, BARBARA
'Pop Art at the Guggenheim', *Art International*, VII: 5. Zurich, May 1963
ROSENBERG, BERNARD and MANNING WHITE, DAVID
Mass Culture, the Popular Arts in America (an anthology). New York, 1957
ROSENBERG, HAROLD
The Anxious Object. New York, 1964
ROSENBLUM, ROBERT
'Roy Lichtenstein', *Metro* 8. Milan, 1962
RUBLOVSKY, JOHN
Pop Art. New York, 1965
SECKLER, D. G.
'Folklore of the Banal', *Art In America*, 4. New York, Winter 1962
SMITH, RICHARD
'New Readers Start Here' (Derek Boshier, David Hockney, Peter Phillips), *Ark* 32. London, Summer 1962
SMITHSON, ALISON AND PETER
'But Today we Collect Ads', *Ark* 18 (the first issue edited by Roger Coleman dealing with popular imagery). London 1956
SOLOMON, ALAN R.
'Jim Dine and the Psychology of the New Art', *Art International*, VIII: 8. Lugano, October 1964
SONTAG, SUSAN
'Notes on "Camp" ', *Partisan Review*, XXXI: 4. New York, Fall 1964
'Pop goes the Easel', The New York Herald Tribune Book Week. New York, July 25, 1965
STEINBERG, LEO
Jasper Johns. New York, 1963
SWENSON, G. R.
'The New American Sign Painters', *Art News*. New York, September 1962
SWENSON, G. R.
'What is Pop Art?' (interviews with Andy Warhol, Robert Indiana, Roy Lichtenstein and Jim Dine), *Art News*. New York, November 1963
SWENSON, G. R.
'What is Pop Art?' (interviews with Jasper Johns, James Rosenquist, Tom Wesselmann, Steve Durkee), *Art News*. New York, February 1964
SYLVESTER, DAVID
'Art in a Coke Climate', *The Sunday Times Colour Magazine*. London, January 26, 1964

TILLIM, SIDNEY
'Month in Review' (Claes Oldenburg and Robert Indiana), *Arts*. New York, Spring 1962
TIMES LITERARY SUPPLEMENT
'Pop Goes the Artist' (a review of *The Popular Arts*, by Stuart Hall and Paddy Whannel, London 1964). London, December 17, 1964
TIMES LITERARY SUPPLEMENT
'Shock Art with a Purpose' (a review of *Dada-Kunst und anti Kunst* by Hans Richter, Cologne 1965). London, February 4, 1965
WOLFRAM, EDDIE
'Pop as Mod', *Art and Artists* I, 1. London, April 1966

Selected Catalogues of Exhibitions

AMSTERDAM, STEDELIJK MUSEUM
'Pop Kunst'. Summer 1964
LONDON, GRABOWSKI GALLERY
'Image in Progress' (including Derek Boshier, David Hockney, Allen Jones and Peter Phillips), by Jasia Reichardt. 1962
LONDON, HANOVER GALLERY
'Slip It To Me', by Richard Hamilton. October 1964
LONDON, INSTITUTE OF CONTEMPORARY ARTS
'The Popular Image' by Alan R. Solomon. October 1963
LONDON, WHITECHAPEL GALLERY
'The New Generation' by David Thompson. March 1964
NEW YORK, GUGGENHEIM MUSEUM
'Six Painters and the Object' by Lawrence Alloway. Bibliography. 1963
NEW YORK, MARLBOROUGH-GERSON GALLERY
'R. B. Kitaj', catalogue notes by the artist. February 1965
NEW YORK, MUSEUM OF MODERN ART
'Americans 1963' (including Claes Oldenburg, Robert Indiana and James Rosenquist), edited by Dorothy Miller. 1963
NEW YORK, SIDNEY JANIS GALLERY
'New Realists' by John Ashbery, S[idney] J[anis] and Pierre Restany. December 1962
MINNEAPOLIS, WALKER ART CENTER
'London: The New Scene' by Martin Friedman and Alan Bowness. Bibliography by Jasia Reichardt. February 1965
PHILADELPHIA INSTITUTE OF CONTEMPORARY ART
'Andy Warhol' by Samuel Adams Green, 1965
STOCKHOLM, MODERNA MUSEET
'Pop Konst Amerikans' by Alan R. Solomon, 1964 (republished in *Art International*, VII: 2, March 1964, as 'New American Art')
VENICE, XXXII ESPOSIZIONE BIENNALE INTERNAZIONALE D'ARTE, AMERICAN PAVILION
'Four Germinal Painters [and] Four Younger Artists' (including Robert Rauschenberg, Jasper Johns, Claes Oldenburg and Jim Dine) by Alan R. Solomon. Summer 1964
WASHINGTON, D.C. THE WASHINGTON GALLERY OF MODERN ART
'The Popular Image Exhibition' by Alan R. Solomon, April 1963 (republished in *Art International*, VII: 7, September 1963, as 'The New Art')

Index to text

Abstract expressionism, 43, 44, 45, 51, 52-3, 71; break from, 51, 103; Dine and, 78; influence of, 28, 43 *et seq*, 71, 78, 85, 141
Abstraction and the representational, 71
Action painting, 92
Advertising, influence of, 11, 12, 17, 19, 31, 43, 57-8, 73, 93-4, 106, 138
Air-brush technique, 21, 132
Albers, Josef, 52
Alloway, Lawrence, 31, 43; invents term 'pop art', 18, 33
America, influence on pop art, 32, 40 *et seq*
Anger, Kenneth, 27
Antonioni, 27
Antrobus, John, 27
Arman, 65, 66
Art, and life, 106; concepts of, 16; division between 'popular' and 'fine', 16, 21; modern view of, 15-6; new definitions of, 66
Artists, changing concepts of, 16
Ashton, Dore, 18
Automatic drawing, 124

Ben Day tints, 88, 126
Blake, Peter, 33, 108 *et seq*; influence of, 34
Boshier, Derek, 34, 39, 131
Buckle, Richard, 33

Cage, John, 29, 30; influence of, 46, 51; *Theory of Inclusion*, 46, 51
Camp, 20, 117

Caulfield, Patrick, 115-6; compared with Lichtenstein, 115
César, 66
Chabaud, 65
Chamberlain, 66
Colour, use of: 20; by Blake, 110; by Caulfield, 116; by Donaldson, 40; by Indiana, 80; by Kitaj, 140; by Laing, 129; by Rosenquist, 94; by Wesselmann, 106
Combines, 51
Comic strip technique, 22, 88, 104, 109, 140
Commercial art, 12; borrowings from, 18, 21
Commonplace, examination of, 18; importance, 55 *et seq;* use of, 19, 66
Conner, 66
Cubists and Cubism, 53, 54, 58, 141
Culture, 15 popular *See* Popular culture

Dada and Dadaists, 54, 55, 66, 79
Dali, Salvadori, 58
Davis, Stuart, 58, 85
Demuth, Charles, 58, 85
Dine, Jim, 45, 46, 63, 78-9, 107
Donaldson, Anthony, 39-40
Duchamp, Marcel, 54, 140; exhibition, 54, 57; influence, 54, 56-7

Environment, 29, 56
Ernst, Max, 55, 58

Fahlstrom, Oyvind, 65
Festa, Tano, 65